Effective Change in Schools

This ⬚ ⬚ is about the management of change in schools. Focusing on resea⬚ ⬚ in schools, the book explores the process of successful and subs⬚ ⬚al educational change. The thirty-two schools which took part in the ⬚ ⬚ all made significant changes in their practice in order to improve pupi⬚ ⬚vement. This book describes and analyses the central features of that ⬚ ⬚ional transformation process.

T⬚ ⬚ includes:

- i⬚ ⬚tion about the project, its aims and purposes
- a⬚ ⬚ and innovative perspective on the change process in schools and t⬚ ⬚ership and management of change
- a⬚ ⬚mination of the key aspects of school effectiveness and i⬚ ⬚ement
- a⬚ ⬚ption of the strategies adopted by the schools to initiate change a⬚ ⬚tline of the issues that the schools faced as they attempted to ⬚ ⬚forward
- a⬚ ⬚sideration of the role of leadership in educational transformation a⬚ ⬚e essence of the successful leader.

This ⬚ ⬚ is grounded in the stories of those who have attempted to bring abou⬚ ⬚cal change in schools. It will inform the experiences and practice of an⬚ ⬚ who is endeavouring to bring about change in their own school or ha⬚ ⬚nterest in educational management and leadership.

Chris ⬚ ⬚s is Professor of Educational Management at the University of Glam⬚ ⬚an Business School. **Una Connolly** is the Project Research Fellow at the University of Glamorgan.

School Leadership Series
Series editors Brent Davies and Linda Ellison

This series bridges the gap between the management handbook approach and the traditional academic text. It provides accessible practitioner-focused leadership that meets the needs of the reflective leader in schools.

It is edited by two experts in the educational leadership field, with a wealth of experience of working with school leaders.

Strategic Direction and Development of the School
Brent Davies and Linda Ellison

School Leadership for the 21st Century
Brent Davies and Linda Ellison

Effective Change in Schools
Chris James and Una Connolly

Effective Change in Schools

Chris James and Una Connolly

London and New York

First published 2000
by RoutledgeFalmer
11 New Fetter Lane, London EC4P 4EE

Simultaneously published in the USA and Canada
by RoutledgeFalmer
29 West 35th Street, New York, NY 10001

RoutledgeFalmer is an imprint of the Taylor & Francis Group

Typeset in Sabon
by Curran Publishing Services Ltd, Norwich
Printed and bound in Great Britain
by University Press, Cambridge

British Library Cataloguing in Publication Data
A catalogue record for this book is available from the British
Library.

Library of Congress Cataloging in Publication Data
James, Chris, 1949–
    Effective change in schools / Chris James and Una Connolly
        p. cm, – (School leadership series)
    Includes bibliographical references and index.
    1. School improvement program –Wales, South–Management–
Case studies. 2. Improving Schools Project–Case studies. 3. School
management and organization–Wales, South–Case studies. I.
Connolly, Una, 1949– II. Title. III Series.

LB2822.84.G7 J26 2000
371.2'009429'4–dc21   00-055331

ISBN 0–415–22190–0 (hbk)
ISBN 0–415–22191–9 (pbk)

Contents

Figures

Tables

Acknowledgements

Our thanks and appreciation go to those colleagues in the schools that were involved in the research on which this book is based. We would like to thank you for two reasons in particular. First, your endeavours in improving the achievements of your pupils have been considerable. There is no better task to be engaged in than improving the life chances of young people. Thank you for your good work. Second, thank you for sharing your experiences and stories with us so openly and honestly. We hope we have done your stories justice. Our thanks and appreciation also go to our families for their love, understanding and patience.

Figure 6.1, Responses to anxiety associated with learning and change, is taken from R. Vince and L. Martin, 'Inside action learning: an exploration of the psychology and politics of the action learning model', in *Management Education and Development*, vol. 24, part 3 (1993), with grateful acknowledgement to Sage Publications Ltd.

Chris James
Una Connolly

1   Introduction

Some background and context

In 1976 the Prime Minister of the time, James Callaghan, made a now famous speech in which he questioned the value for money of the British education system. He set in motion what was called 'The Great Debate' in which the contribution of the education system to national well-being was opened up to scrutiny. Callaghan initiated an era of accountability for education, and since that time Britain has demanded more from its schools. Although this increased accountability has been lived out in a number of ways and taken on a number of different guises in the last twenty-five years, there is no doubt that it has placed an imperative on schools continually to change in order to improve. As a result, change management has become almost axiomatic in the leadership and management of educational organisations. The management of educational change is, in essence, what this book is about.

In the contemporary setting, the management of educational institutions exposes schools to the three sharp prongs of the so-called 'new public management'. The first of these is the establishment of a quasi-market in education which exposes schools to 'market type mechanisms'. In this increasingly diverse market, parental choice (or perhaps more appropriately, parental preference), open enrolment, age-weighted pupil funding, and a mixture of different kinds of schools in any locality are all intended to engender a climate of competition. In this competitive arena, there is a pressure on schools to be effective and to improve their effectiveness so that they maintain their competitive advantage.

The second element of new public management for schools is the decentralisation of power and control, and the creation of institutional autonomy where individual schools are encouraged and enabled to function on their own and manage their own budgets. Within this institutional and financial autonomy, and the freedom it creates – albeit a freedom constrained by some fairly tight central controls and parameters – schools are expected to optimise the use of their own resources, to flourish and to improve.

The third element of the new public management for schools is performance management, where the work of schools is monitored and made public. This scrutiny of performance is achieved through inspection by central government agencies, for example OFSTED in England and ESTYN in Wales, and the publication of output measures of effectiveness in 'league tables' of the pupils' examination results. These purport to give a measure of schools' performance, albeit a very simple and somewhat unsophisticated one, in the context of a standardised 'national' curriculum.

The final piece of this policy jigsaw is about to be implemented at the time of writing. That is the performance management of teachers, where individual teachers are rewarded for their (and their pupils') performance.

It has to be said that in the early days of this era of educational accountability, some schools needed to change. Over time, there is no doubt that some schools, for a variety of reasons, were not giving their pupils the kind of educational experience that many other (often neighbouring) schools were able to provide. Also some schools were under-performing and needed to change quite substantially and very quickly. There is also a very good case for arguing that the whole process of teaching and learning in schools had become hidden and impenetrable. By and large it had become known and understood only by the teaching profession itself. Opening up the work of schools to greater public scrutiny has forced many schools to improve the quality of many aspects of their activities. Also, schools have been exposed to other trends in the non-educational world, such as quality management and the growing importance of communicating with and responding to the needs of the customer.

In parallel with and closely related to the development of increased accountability, there has been a greater interest in the whole notion of improving schools. The so-called school improvement movement is a wide grouping which embraces a number of different strands. These include school effectiveness, the management of change, and educational leadership. More recently, the focus has shifted towards the processes of teaching and learning in schools, and the creation of internal conditions which enable continual change and improvement. One of the particular strengths of the school improvement movement is that it has provided a vehicle for exploring what schools do and identifying ways of improving practice. It is also an international movement, and although there are difficulties in transferring practices from one cultural context to another, there is no doubt that alternative perspectives can be helpful in considering the most appropriate ways of changing practice in order to improve pupil achievement.

Another pressure on schools to change lies in the complex interplay between the nature of society and the work of schools. At the beginning of the twenty-first century, we appear to be living in times of unprecedented change, and schools must change rapidly in response. Of course, some may argue that the pace of change always appears to be rapid for any generation or in any time period. There is always a problem with judging the pace of change. The difficulty lies in the fact that the extent of change and its pace are largely subjectively and individually experienced. Reliable and valid objective indicators of the pace of social change are difficult to come by. However, there can be little doubt that many aspects of life are changing radically. These changes are driven in large measure by the new information and communication technologies which have integrated and increased data storage, retrieval and display capacity, miniaturisation, portability and ease of communication. But these new technologies are not the only factor. There have been changes in the structure of society, in the working lives of women and in the nature of work generally. The globalisation of economies is also changing the nature of the business and commercial world. And all of these changes, are taking place in the wider context of the impact of human activity on the environment. All these changes and the pace of change, have placed an imperative on schools to change what they do and how they do it.

Perhaps unfortunately for schools, the requirement to undertake educational change has coincided with a realisation of the complexity and hence the problematic nature of educational change. Change in schools *is* mostly difficult and complicated. It *is not* often easy and simple. There *is* a good case for arguing that the leadership and management of change in schools require a sophisticated approach, considerable skill and, in many cases, resolute determination. None the less, successful change does take place all the time in schools, and many schools have the capacity to change to improve the educational achievements and subsequent life chances of their pupils. It was to explore these successful change processes in schools, to analyse the factors that influence them, and to disseminate to a wider audience some of these lessons of change, that the research that underpins the substance of this book was started.

The Improving Schools Project was undertaken in South Wales in the area formerly known as Mid Glamorgan, which now comprises the local education authorities of Bridgend, Caerphilly, Merthyr Tydfil and Rhondda-Cynon-Taff. These are the neighbouring authorities of the University of Glamorgan where the project was based. The project was supported financially and also in purpose and practice by the university, the local authorities and ESIS, the Education Support and Inspection Service. ESIS is the former Mid Glamorgan Advisory Service, which was retained intact after local government reorganisation in March 1996. Essential and important partners in the project were of course the thirty-two schools involved. They were invited to join the project on the basis that they had changed their practices in order to bring about improved pupil achievement, or were attempting to do so.

The contents of the book

In this book we have attempted to explore the process of successful and substantial educational change. It has become clear to us that much of the educational process, and therefore the process of changing it, is not always understandable or explainable in a rational way. Although there may be a surface rationality to it all, there are often very powerful non-rational, emotional forces at work. It is from that perspective that we have attempted to make sense of, and to theorise about, the educational change process.

Following this introductory chapter, the second chapter gives some additional information about the project, and in particular its aims and purposes. Chapter 2 also gives some outline information on the schools that participated in the project and the areas in which they are situated. It outlines the preliminary findings of the first part of the project's work, which explored the ways in which the schools considered that they had changed. This data collection was for us an important first stage in making contact with the schools and establishing working relationships with them. As we explain in the chapter, this preliminary exploration also gave us a basis on which to choose schools for further in-depth study. The ways in which the schools considered that they had changed ranged from process measures to output indicators of improved pupil achievement.

Chapter 3 gives a brief overview of organisational change and in particular the nature of change in educational organisations. The literature on change is complex and inter-connected, and this brief overview is structured in the following way. The first section outlines why change in educational institutions is so complex. The next section continues this theme and considers some aspects of the management of change in general terms. There are then two sections, the first of which explores some frameworks and guidelines for managing organisational change, while the second describes some models for understanding change. Because leadership and change are so inextricably linked there is next a section that explores different aspects of leadership. A final section to the chapter briefly explores the key themes in school effectiveness and improvement.

One of the particular challenges of exploring change is to create a framework within which to make sense of all the various events, happenings, responses, actions and reactions to the change process. We have deliberately chosen to view the findings from the point of view of what we are calling 'institutional transformation'. We outline this institutional transformation perspective in Chapter 4. There are two main themes in this perspective which, importantly, are linked. The first theme essentially embraces the non-rational emotional responses of individuals and institutions. This psychodynamic perspective therefore includes the influence of the unconscious, the defences of individuals and institutions against emotional pain, and the ways in which groups behave (group relations). The second major theme is open systems theory, which provides a useful way of thinking about individuals and groups and their roles in institutions. These two perspectives link together in the particular challenge that taking up and enacting a role has for individuals and institutions. (In this book, we argue that it is the particular role of leadership to enable individuals and institutions to take up and enact their roles.) The combination of these two perspectives is crucial, since the open systems theory perspective helps the understanding and resolution of the issues revealed by the psychodynamic perspective.

In order to make overall sense of the changes that the schools have undergone, we have modelled the changes into three phases: a pre-acceleration phase, an acceleration phase and a post-acceleration phase. Chapter 5 describes the characteristics of the schools in the pre-acceleration phase and outlines some of the challenges that the schools faced as they started their school improvement journeys. Many of these will have a familiar ring to them, and taken together they are a formidable list. Thankfully, none of the schools suffered from all of the problems (although, of course, many of the difficulties were linked and therefore came together), and importantly all of the schools in the project were overcoming the problems, or had overcome the problems and moved on.

Chapter 6 describes the strategies adopted by the schools to initiate change, and outlines some of the issues that the schools faced as they attempted to move forward. Chapter 7 describes the nature of the schools and the leadership of the schools as changes were implemented. We have called this stage the acceleration phase because of the climate created within the schools as changes, which were often multifarious in nature and widespread in scope, were initiated. Chapter 8 is the last in this group, and describes the change processes in the schools. Schools successfully entering this post-acceleration stage appear to take on a more strategic approach to the change process, where their actions are more long-term, considered and deliberate. This chapter, which has as its main title 'Going strategic', describes some of the main themes in the management and organisation of the schools in this stage of their improvement journey.

A dominant theme in the change literature and in the literature on good schools is that of leadership. Generally, the literature on leadership implicitly accepts that leadership is an essential requirement for a fully functioning institution (although it has to be said that there is a countervailing view). The importance of leadership emerged in this study too, and for that reason we have chosen to devote Chapter 9 to a consideration of leadership. The chapter first discusses the preliminary ideas about leadership that emerged from the study. The following part seeks to analyse these further into a set of leadership principles that outline the essence of leadership as it has emerged for us in the literature and in the findings of the research. The principles, with the helpful acronym of 'LEADER', provide a framework for consideration of the different aspects of leadership. The key principles of ensuring *Effectiveness*, optimising *Reflectivity* and optimising Adaptability also have a useful acronym in this *era* of leadership in which we are apparently living, especially in the world of education.

In the final chapter, Chapter 10, we briefly re-examine the institutional transformation perspective and consider the implications for its use in understanding educational institutions and for supporting the effective management of change in schools. We also set out some important characteristics of leadership, which perhaps go further than the list of the attributes of leaders and leadership that we identified in the project in Chapter 9, and which add to the leadership principles. These aspects include the central role of emotion in organising; the special nature of the leadership role in organisations; the leadership role in the containment of individual and institutional anxiety; and leadership as organisational integration. It also includes an exploration of what may underpin the vision apparently possessed by so many of the leaders of educational change in our study, and the determination with which we found they pursued their leadership task. The text section of the book ends with an appendix that gives details of the work of the project in promoting collaboration.

In this book, we have kept the number of cited texts and journal articles to a minimum. This action has been deliberate. Of course we want the book to be credible to an academic audience, and referencing those sources where assertions have their grounding and where the evidence for them is to be found is an important way of achieving that. However, we want most of all for the book to be useful and helpful to all those who work to change and improve schools. To that end – and on the advice of colleagues in schools – we have attempted to avoid the use of references except where we thought they were particularly important, and where they refer to a particular idea, theory or finding. To explain the origins of the ideas in this book and to suggest useful further reading, there is an annotated bibliography at the end of the text. This bibliography lists and outlines the content of a number of texts which have influenced our thinking, and which readers of this book will almost certainly find useful.

2 The Improving Schools Project

Introduction

The findings on which this book is based resulted from a research project located in South Wales at the University of Glamorgan. The project, which had the title of the Improving Schools Project, began in October 1996 and ended (its first phase at least) in September 1998. In that time the project researched the changes that thirty-two local schools had implemented to improve pupil achievement. This chapter describes the work of the project.

The chapter begins by describing the overall context of the project, outlining the project's aims and describing those schools, authorities and other institutions that contributed to the work. The section that follows describes the methodology, research design, and the data collection and analysis methods. The work was broadly in two phases. The first stage, which was largely exploratory, is described in this chapter and the findings outlined. The research process of the second more substantial phase is then described. The findings of this second phase are detailed in Chapters 5, 6, 7 and 8. This chapter ends with an outline of the dissemination work of the project.

The project

The Improving Schools Project was launched in October 1996 following an initial planning and preparation phase which began during the late spring of 1996. The project was a collaboration between the University of Glamorgan, the education authorities of Bridgend, Caerphilly, Merthyr Tydfil and Rhondda-Cynon-Taff, and ESIS, the Education, Support and Inspection Service for the four authorities. The Welsh Secondary Schools Association (WSSA) gave advice which was valuable in setting up and subsequently supporting the project. The early planning established the project's overall aims, which were to research the changes that had been implemented in local schools in order to improve the educational achievement of pupils, and to contribute to the development and dissemination of good practice.

Una Connolly, the project Research Fellow, carried out the bulk of the data collection and analysis, assisted in the second stage by Jean Williams and Nesta James. Professor Chris James was responsible for the overall direction of the project's research work. The project's work was guided and supported by an advisory committee which comprised representatives of the university, the local education authorities, the WSSA, and three former members of the Office of Her Majesty's Chief Inspector of Schools in Wales.

The first and substantive aim of the project was to explore, analyse and document changes in practice that had contributed to the improvements claimed by the schools. In setting out to achieve this aim, we recognised that in their work to improve pupil achievement individual schools face different challenges, and their capacities for change vary. Those in *ex officio* leadership positions in the schools – the headteachers, deputy head teachers, and heads of department/curriculum co-ordinators – have different leadership styles and use different change management strategies. As a consequence (and as one might expect) there are many versions of change and improvement, some of which have been more successful than others. It is unlikely therefore that the improvement processes used by individual schools, operating within their own contexts, will provide a detailed blueprint for other schools to replicate. However, the intention was to contribute to knowledge and understanding of the processes of change in educational organisations by developing some overarching theories and principles which would be widely applicable and useful. It was further hoped that the sharing of these ideas and accounts of successful practice among schools within the individual local education authorities and across authority boundaries would make a useful contribution to improving educational achievement. In the Welsh context, the White Paper *Building Excellent Schools Together* (Welsh Office 1997), with its emphasis on the need for those committed to raising standards to work together, gave the collaborative purpose of the project a welcome and timely boost.

The initial planning of the project took place during the spring and summer terms of 1996. It was agreed that the project should have research and development/dissemination phases, although it was recognised that these would not be – and probably should not be – separate and distinct. It was decided that the work of the project would be in three stages.

1   (Following the initial planning) a preliminary preparation stage. The schools identified were visited to make initial contact, and to begin the collection of evidence to establish the nature and validity of the claims for improved practice. These visits were also an opportunity to gather contextual information about the schools.
2   The schools were revisited in order to collect detailed information, which was used to characterise the change processes.

3   In the third and overlapping stage, the project worked to disseminate successful school improvement practice.

A number of principles underpinned the research work of the project.

- From the outset the project was concerned to promote a spirit of collaboration with colleagues in schools. It wished to be seen as researching *with* colleagues rather than researching *on* colleagues.
- The project also wished to be seen as *celebrating* good practice rather than being perceived as *evaluating* practice.
- Many of the schools with which the project worked have made significant progress along the school improvement pathway. They had undergone significant change in order to improve pupil achievement. The project's work was to understand the steps taken on that journey, so that others might learn from them.
- The project was concerned to ground the research findings in the teachers' and educational managers' own experience. It was also keen to report the factors that influenced change, and that were of significance to those involved in the change process. We hoped that this overall strategy would enhance the value of the findings to colleagues in other schools.
- Finally, the project hoped to contribute to establishing a theoretical understanding of the change process in schools. We hoped that this theoretical basis would enable aspects of educational change to be understood better by those experiencing change in schools. We also hoped that this basis would help those seeking to manage change to act more appropriately and with greater insight.

The schools involved in the project

Thirty-two schools were involved in the project. They included infant, junior, primary, secondary and special schools. Four of the schools were Welsh-medium schools, that is, schools where Welsh is the language of communication in most aspects of school life and the main medium of learning. The four local authorities undertook the selection of thirty schools for inclusion in the project. The schools were chosen predominantly on the grounds that they were making, or had made, significant changes in their practice in order to enhance pupil achievement. Some schools were included, quite appropriately, because there were clear signs that interesting developments were taking place and that these developments would be facilitated by involvement in the project. The authorities agreed to the request of a further two schools who wished to participate in the project.

Three of the four unitary authorities, Bridgend, Caerphilly and Rhondda-Cynon-Taff, chose to include both primary and secondary schools in the first phase of the project. Merthyr Tydfil was unique in including all of its five secondary schools. Two special schools, one located in the Bridgend and one in the Merthyr Tydfil authority, were involved. Their inclusion usefully widened the scope of the project, as both schools cater for pupils with a wide range of learning difficulties in the primary and secondary age groups.

The area that the schools serve is mixed in socio-economic terms. It is the part of Wales which was formerly home to the South Wales coal mining industry. That industry has all but gone now, and the region is undergoing economic restructuring and regeneration. There is no doubt that parts of this region are seriously disadvantaged economically, and therefore to an extent socially. But the stereotypical view of this area, especially the 'Valleys' communities, as one of uniform socioeconomic disadvantage is neither true nor fair.

The first phase of the project

The purpose of the first phase of the research was to make initial individual contact with the schools and to begin the collection of evidence to establish the nature and validity of the claims for improved practice. This section outlines the methods employed in this first stage and describes the findings. There is also a brief section which discusses the outcomes.

The research in the first phase

In the preliminary first stage, all thirty-two schools were visited. The first visit was to establish and begin building relationships particularly with the headteachers. It also enabled us to provide assurances about the confidentiality of data collected throughout the period of the project. Semi-structured interviews were conducted in each of the schools with the headteacher on her/his own and, on occasions, with a deputy headteacher. In two of the local authorities, a senior member of the local education authority accompanied the researcher on these initial visits. This arrangement provided a useful introduction for both the researcher and the school.

Prepared questions were used to help focus discussion on the key areas in which the school felt it had achieved significant improvement. The use of these questions, however, did not restrict the responses of those interviewed. The respondents were encouraged to provide general background information about the school. They were also encouraged to raise in discussion anything they felt was a significant factor in the change process. The headteachers were also asked to identify which factors they felt had contributed to the achievement of improvements, and to distinguish and characterise those factors that had hindered or were still hindering progress. Almost all of these interviews were tape-recorded with the approval of those concerned, and transcripts prepared.

The schools were asked to provide evidence to support their claimed improvements. This evidence was varied in nature, but was typically quantitative. For example, they provided National Curriculum assessment results, external examination results, information on pupil attendance and exclusions and the destination of school leavers. Some schools also made available background indicators such as the proportion of pupils with special educational needs and those entitled to free school meals. Documentary evidence was provided by the schools to support their claims for improvement in a range of areas. They were able to supply reports of external audits, such as general inspection reports and reviews of specific aspects of their provision undertaken by the local-authority-funded Educational Support and Inspection Service (ESIS); these identified the school's strengths and weaknesses. Other documentary evidence included post-inspection action plans, school development plans, school prospectuses and internal documents that highlighted how particular areas had developed over a period of time. On completion of the first phase of data collection, the interview transcripts and the documentary evidence were categorised, coded and analysed.

The findings of the first phase

During the data collection, the headteachers identified almost fifty factors that related to change and improvement. These factors are illustrated in Table 2.1. The table also records the number of times each aspect was cited in the initial interviews.

The factors identified by the schools were diverse and wide-ranging. This finding is interesting in itself, and gives an indication of the complexity of the change processes that need to be carried through as schools strive to improve pupil achievement. One headteacher summed up the views of many others:

> One doesn't really know what is working and what is working for individual children. We have to set up things on all fronts, to pull a lot of levers, but keep the goal in view.

During the data analysis, no attempt was made to restrict or frame the respondents' interpretation of these factors into input, process or output/outcome indicators of performance. Although the factors cited are diverse, the most frequent are not unexpected given what is known generally about improving practice. The wide range of changes made in some schools is interesting, with a number of schools carrying through a very wide range indeed. The pace and extent of change in these schools clearly was, or had been, considerable, as the follow up in-depth case studies indicated.

Table 2.1 Factors identified by headteachers in order of number of times cited

Code	Description	Number of times cited
LP	Improved links with parents	30
SI	Increased staff involvement in whole school planning/decision making	29
CPH	Changes in personnel: new headteacher or other senior staff member	27
IC	More effective channels of communication within the school	27
SD	More focused staff development	26
TA	Stronger team approach	26
TL	Stronger focus on teaching and learning	26
RR	New and more clearly defined staff roles and responsibilities	25
LS	Improved links with other schools	25
LC	Improved links with the community	24
CP	Changes in personnel: other staff	24
E	Higher expectations	24
L	Strong leadership	23
SA	Improved standards of achievement	22
M	More effective monitoring	21
E	More effective evaluation	21
PSE	Increased pupil self-esteem	20
LE	Improvements to the learning environment	20
CC	Changes in school climate/learning conditions	19
PP	Increased pupil participation	19
SM	Improved staff morale	19
PA	Improved pupil attendance	17
ARR	More effective use of assessment information and of recording and reporting	16
TS	More effective use of target setting	15
LG	Improved links with governors	15
MS	Improved management structures	14
VG	Clear vision and goals	14
D	Improved standards of behaviour/discipline	14
EXC	Improved provision and attendance at extra-curricular activities	13
RES	Improved resources	13
SS	Improved pupil support mechanisms, for example, study support	12
RW	Increased use of reward systems	12
PAT	Improvement in pupils' attitudes	11
CE	Improved curriculum entitlement	11
SEN	Improvements to provision for pupils with Special Educational Needs	11
MR	Improved management/staff relationships	10
PS	More effective pastoral support	9
MIS	More effective use of information systems	9
PN	Increase in pupil numbers	8
RoA	More effective use of pupils' Records of Achievement	7
ICO	Improved classroom organisation	6

Table 2.1 continued

Code	Description	Number of times cited
B	Improved budgetary/financial control	6
QT	Improved quality of teaching	5
LIT	Improvements in standards of literacy	5
IiP	Benefits of Investors in People	5
PE	Increase in the number of pupils entered for public examinations	3
ER	Fewer exclusions	2
ES	Availability of experienced supply staff	2
ITT	Benefits of involvement in initial teacher training	1

The second phase of the project

Following the first stage of the project, further visits were made to all thirty-two schools to explore in detail the nature of the change process that had taken place. A number of schools were subsequently chosen for more in-depth study. This section describes the methods used in this second stage. The findings are detailed in Chapters 5, 6, 7 and 8.

The research

It was evident from initial discussions with headteachers that many of the schools had either achieved significant improvements, or made changes that would in all probability lead towards improved pupil achievement. However, it was equally evident that some of the schools have travelled further than others in their 'school improvement journey'. Since in-depth study of all the schools would have been difficult given the very limited resources available it was necessary to select a smaller number of schools on which to focus detailed data collection.

The selection of these schools was based on the claims made for improvement in key areas identified by the headteachers, and on contextual factors. At least two schools were selected in each local authority. Schools were included which represented the range of educational provision across the authorities. Approximately one-sixth of the schools involved in the project had recently been formed through the merger of other schools. These 'merged schools' often face particular problems in their quest for improvement, so it was decided to represent them in the sample for further research. Ten schools were selected on the basis of these criteria, and these became known as the case-study schools. Much of the data presented in the book comes from these case study schools.

From the outset, the project was established to research the changed and changing practices that had contributed to improved achievement in the view of those in the schools. The practitioners' perceptions of what had happened, what worked and what was not so successful were important, as were their stories of improvement. These perceptions, the successes and failures and the accounts of those involved in bringing about change, gave a valuable representation of the journey travelled by the schools. Stories and recollections from a number of sources, including the headteacher, other teachers, parents, governors and pupils, provided a rich set of data. The overall intention of the data gathering and analysis was to build a vivid and authentic picture that would make the findings:

- *credible* in that the accounts of the change processes would be believable
- *transferable* in that the analysis and interpretations would be exchangeable and interchangeable with others' experience and findings
- *dependable* in that the findings and the analysis could be relied upon
- *confirmable* in the sense that researching the respondents' experience again would reveal a broadly similar picture.

The schools studied were at various stages in their development, and their accounts enabled us to build a picture of the pathway of the process of improvement.

Data collection in the case-study schools involved further semi-structured interviews, not only with the headteachers but also with teaching staff at various levels in the school. Where possible, pupils and parents were interviewed. In some cases governors were also interviewed. Questioning focused on clarifying the nature of the changes achieved, and in particular on the change process. Opening questions included the following.

- Why was change in this area necessary?
- Who was involved in prioritising areas for development?
- How much support and commitment for change was there at the time of initiation?
- How was change brought about? What strategies were used?
- What factors were identified as inhibiting/facilitating change?
- How was resistance to change overcome?
- How were the priorities for development communicated to others?
- Were governors/pupils/parents involved in developmental activities? In what way?
- What resources were required to implement change?
- How does the school ensure implementation of changes and sustain momentum?
- What is the key dynamic necessary for effective and sustained development leading to improvement?
- What advice would you give to others who need to make similar change?

In pursuing and probing responses, we asked the respondents to give specific examples to illustrate the point they were making in their answer, and to give reasons for making the response. On occasions they indicated that they would prefer particular aspects to remain confidential. We appreciated the sharing of such information, as it often shed useful light on the improvement process in a particular school. The interviews were tape-recorded with the consent of the interviewees, and subsequently transcribed for analysis. This data analysis was carried out using standard qualitative data analysis methods that involved summarising and coding the data. Emergent themes were identified and developed.

Facilitating inter-school collaboration and the sharing of good practice

This section describes some of the work of the project in encouraging the sharing of good practice and disseminating the results.

An important aim of the project was to promote and facilitate the sharing of experience *among* schools as they strove to improve pupils' progress and achievements. The journeys of improvement confirmed the very complex nature of schools as organisations. Of equal complexity are the factors contributing to successful change in order to enhance pupil achievement. The sharing of good practice is problematic for a number of reasons, most notably the competitive climate that has been created by successive government policies. In considering competition and collaboration between schools, there appears to be a paradox at work. At one and the same time, schools are expected to compete, and to collaborate and share good practice. There is increasing pressure on schools to improve and to deliver higher standards for pupils. As a result there are both competitive pressures and collaborative pressures.

Competitive pressures can be encapsulated as follows: a good reputation means more pupils and hence (financial) survival, as well as enhanced promotion prospects for headteachers and other senior managers. Collaborative pressures can be summarised thus: teachers wish to see all pupils perform to the highest standards, and are willing both to pass on their own experiences and to learn from other teachers. The result is that schools from the same area compete and collaborate at the same time, generating tensions between those pressures *for*, and those which *inhibit* or limit, collaboration and inter-school working. The sharing of professional knowledge, arguably a central part of good professional practice, is often restricted in practice. So, as a general statement it is probably true to say that the sharing of knowledge and understanding has not been as widespread as it could have been.

The work undertaken by the project to promote and enhance collaboration is outlined in Appendix 1.

3   Educational change

Introduction

Change is an interesting notion. It is all around us, within us, and it is difficult if not impossible to escape from it. Change is perpetual. We might like to think we have at some time a period of stability but change carries on none the less. Just by living we experience change, if only because we grow older. Change can be minor, low key and easily handled. It can however be substantial, very significant and extremely difficult to cope with. Change may be started by others and imposed upon us, or we may initiate it and carry it through ourselves. At one level, it is simple. Change is simply a matter of learning to do things differently. But in reality it is extremely complex, especially if the change is significant.

This chapter explores some of the issues that relate to change in general, and educational change in particular. It begins with a section that 'thinks out loud' about why change in educational institutions is so complex. The next section looks at some of the perspectives on the management of change. A subsequent section examines what we know about leadership. The final section briefly explores the notions of change in educational settings, and in particular briefly addresses the issues of school improvement and effectiveness.

The real complexity of change in educational institutions

Change is complex because it is inextricably linked to our emotions. Imposed change can call up a whole range of emotions: anger at the imposition and the denial of personal autonomy, sorrow at the sense of loss of the old, and anxiety at the uncertainties that the new will bring. Self-initiated change is also intertwined with emotion: excitement at the anticipation of the new, relief that the old will be left behind, and again anxiety because of the uncertainty and the unknown events that have been set in motion. Anxiety is likely to be the dominant emotion in the management of both imposed and self-initiated change. It will be there in its own right, but it will also be present because experiencing emotions, or even the prospect of experiencing emotions, can cause anxiety. As we explore in the next chapter, we seek to defend ourselves against anxiety and other emotions, because we anticipate a recurrence of the pain that unpleasant feelings have caused us in the past. We may therefore be so well defended against anxiety that we do not recognise it in the change process. Emotional responses are essentially non-rational by definition, although we might like to think that we have a rational understanding and control of them. The management of these non-rational responses to change, especially anxiety, is crucial in change management.

There is a case for arguing that schools are organisations built for the management of change. The logic of this statement is as follows. The central purpose of educational institutions is to manage learning. To learn is to change, hence the role of schools in managing change. It is of course that change/learning management purpose which makes schools special kinds of organisations. They are in a sense learning organisations, but perhaps not in the way in which the term 'learning organisation' is used in contemporary management and organisation literature. The idea of a learning organisation is that learning is built into organisational processes but learning may not be the central institutional purpose.

Since change, learning and emotions are inextricably linked, schools are places where the management of emotions is important. Those who work in educational organisations have to stir up emotions in order to generate a desire to learn in the learners, and to motivate them. They have to manage the emotions concerned with the process of learning. They have to manage the emotions that result from the outcomes of learning. The way in which teachers manage emotions, especially anxiety, is to contain them. They create and act as a holding place, a container, for any anxieties about learning that the learner cannot cope with and wishes to project elsewhere. In this educating/anxiety containment role, educators develop a whole set of coping strategies. These are the rituals and routines of educational organisations.

The problem with the management of change in educational institutions is that it can involve a change in the anxiety-containing processes. So the management of change in educational institutions is likely to involve managing non-rational responses to changes to an existing system for managing non-rational responses. It is this complicating factor that gives us the 'double whammy' of educational change. For example, a teacher may have a set of well-established classroom routines for teaching a particular topic or cross-curricular skill, such as reading. This framework helps to structure the learning process and to contain the emotion associated with learning. If the curriculum is changed or a new teaching method is imposed, those routines have to be changed and a new set put in place to act as the emotional container. Providing the secure framework for containing the emotional dimension of the task of learning is important for teachers.

Without it their authority as teachers is undermined. This issue is most apparent when, for example, teachers are asked to teach outside their subject area, or to use computers in their teaching when they are unfamiliar with them. Because of the lack of familiarity they are unable to provide a framework or structure to contain the emotional dimension of the learning task, and their authority as teachers is impaired. So in educational change, there is both change in the process and change in the way in which we manage (consciously and unconsciously) the emotional dimension of the process in the classroom. The situation is made yet worse because change that is initiated to improve pupil achievement is likely to involve taking a risk. At a fundamental level, this risk is to the life chances of the pupils for which the teacher is responsible. We can never be certain that a proposed educational change will work and benefit the pupils. This additional factor may impose an additional emotional burden that may in turn cause further anxiety.

The management of change

The management of change has been the subject of much study and investigation. Rather than attempting to set out and explain all that is known about change, this section looks at some of the key themes and models in the change literature. We have attempted to point to the landmarks in the terrain rather than provide a detailed map. The section first explores the nature of change generally, in order to explain why change is difficult to manage and understand. It then briefly reviews sources of resistance to change in organisations. Working with resistance to change is one of the key leadership tasks in change management. The section then looks at frameworks and guidance for change management which have been provided by different authors and theorists. The final part of the section outlines models for understanding and analysing the change process.

The nature of change

Morrison (1998) provides a very useful analysis of the main themes in the recent literature on educational change and the management of educational change. He identifies the main themes as follows.

- *Change is structural and systemic.* Any real change will affect the whole system, in that change in one part of an institution has a knock-on effect in other parts. If the change is substantial, it is not likely to be singular and simple; it is more likely to be composite and complex in nature, involving other areas of the organisation.
- *Change is a process that occurs over time.* Because any change takes place over time, organisational change is not a discrete event, it is not sequential and it does not follow a straight line.

- *Change is multi-dimensional.* Change encompasses a number of different dimensions including resources; content; process; evaluation; leadership; management; administration; knowledge; attitudes; emotions; beliefs; values and principles.
- *Change is viewed differently by the various participants and therefore calls up a range of responses.* All those involved in the change process will have their own perspective on it. Change is experienced at both the personal and institutional levels, and the experience of change is heavily influenced by the context.
- *Change management requires investment in technological resources, human resources and the management of the process.* The effective management of change requires creativity and the ability to identify and solve problems.
- *Change strategies must emerge over time, be flexible and adaptive.* The management of change needs to integrate change efforts from the top and bottom of the organisation.

Responses to change

The initiation of change will be both rational and non-rational, and responses to it will be likewise. People and systems respond to change both in a logical way and in a way which is clearly underpinned by emotions. Connor (1995) lists the main reasons for resisting change. They are as follows.

- *Lack of trust.* People may resist change because they do not trust the motives of those proposing it. Those individuals who are resisting change may not trust the change initiators' interpretation of the need for change. Those resisting a proposed change may feel that it has hidden, ominous and serious consequences that will only become apparent at a later time.
- *Belief that change is unnecessary.* If there is no clear evidence that the need for change is high, then resistance will also be high. Even if the need for change is recognised, the inclination will be to change current practice incrementally rather than to go for a more radical change in practice.
- *Belief that change is not feasible.* Although the need for change may be recognised, resistance to it may be justified on the grounds that the proposed change will not work. Failure of earlier change initiatives will increase cynicism about future ones.
- *Economic threats.* Proposed change is likely to be resisted if it threatens the job security of those affected by it. This threat could be perceived in a number of ways. Changes in ways of working might make existing skill sets redundant. Changes in structure may make particular posts redundant. The change may signal a shift, the future implications of which may affect job security.

- *The relatively high cost.* In any change the benefits can be set against the costs. As many of the costs and benefits will be contentious and a matter for debate, the cost/benefit equation can be used to resist change.
- *Fear of failure.* Change requires adaptation to a new way of working. The anxieties that individuals may have about their capability to adapt may cause resistance to change. They may also be anxious that they will not be as effective in the new situation as they are at present.
- *Loss of status and power.* Institutional change almost inevitably results in a change in the institutional hierarchy, the 'pecking order'. Existing networks of influence may be disturbed by a change in the structure of the system. The prospect of these disruptions may provoke resistance to change.
- *Threats to values and ideals.* Change that is not consistent with individuals' values and beliefs is likely to be strongly resisted. This kind of threat can be perceived as a threat to individuals' integrity and their sense of self.
- *Resentment of interference.* Some people will resist a change if they see it as an attempt to be controlled by others. Members of the institution who have low self-esteem may seek to give themselves confidence and security by remaining firmly in control of their world. They are likely strongly to resist any disturbance to the structures they have put in place to ensure this security.

It is important to view these resistances as natural responses. They are understandable because at the heart of them all is emotion, especially anxiety. As discussed earlier in this chapter, this anxiety will be greater if the change seeks to alter the social defences that have been put in place to defend against anxiety. All these resistances are held with conviction; they are active and have energy. Some writers consider that rather than seeing resistances as something to be battered down, the energy of resistance should be redirected to improve change. There is no doubt that the energy of the resistance will become a powerful force for commitment to the change if conversion is possible. The problem is that the capacity for adaptability needs to be encouraged all the time. It is not something to be worked upon only at times of change. It may be too late then, and the inability to adapt and to be flexible may be an insurmountable obstacle. Encouraging adaptability needs to be worked upon much earlier. As we discuss in Chapter 9, encouraging optimum levels of adaptability is a key leadership task.

Action research, problem solving and change

Action research, especially collaborative action research, can be very powerful in achieving organisational change. As a mode of enquiry, action research covers a broad range of approaches. In essence, action research involves the researcher working on a matter that is of genuine concern to the individual and/or the organisation. Ideally the researcher works with members of the organisation where the research is taking place. There should be a genuine intention to take action based on the intervention in order to improve practice.

Although that definition sounds complicated, the main point is that action research has three key features: the 'three I's' of intervention, involvement and improvement.

1   *Intervention.* Action research involves making an intervention of some kind into the organisational processes with a view to changing those processes.
2   *Involvement.* In action research the researcher or researchers are involved in the intervention. The researchers are not separate, objective observers of the intervention. They are part of it.
3   *Improvement.* The intervention is made with an intention of changing practice so as to improve it in some way.

A further key feature is that at all stages the research is engaged in reflectively by all those involved. At all stages of the intervention – the change initiative – there is reflection. So there needs to be a continual process of action followed by reflection that is followed by further action and further reflection and so on.

Action research for educational improvement typically has a problem-solving orientation. Some authors, for example Jean McNiff (1988) and Jack Whitehead (1989), suggest that the intervention and the research into it are shaped in terms of a problem to be solved. Stating the research issue as a problem-solving question can focus the problem or professional concern. So, for a science teacher the question might be:

How do I improve my use of groupwork in my science teaching?

A head of humanities might pose herself the question:

How do I improve the way in which I communicate with members of my faculty?

For the headteacher of a primary school the question could be:

How do I improve the way I communicate with the parents of the pupils in my school?

Questions of this kind are useful because they place the individual at the centre of the process, and because they focus on improvements in practice. Although the individual is central, the intervention cannot be considered without a recognition of the context. Also, collaborative approaches to action research, where a group may be collectively attempting to improve their practice are likely to be more helpful and productive. The reason the involvement of others is crucial is that a change by one member of the organisation will require a change in others to accommodate it.

Action research is inevitably seen as cyclical – as indeed are all problem-solving strategies – because the process of solving one problem usually reveals others. The action research cycle was first developed by Kurt Lewin in the 1940s (Jones 1968, Kanter, Stein and Jick 1992) and has been developed considerably since. The model advocated by Jean McNiff illustrates the main features of an action research cycle. The cycle is broadly similar to problem-solving strategies advocated by many authors for use by managers of change. Indeed some action research theorists, in explaining the process of action research for the management of organisational change, clearly assert the importance of starting with a problem.

A generalised model of action research that draws on the work of the main action research theorists is shown in Figure 3.1. The stages of the action research enquiry are as follows.

1   The identification of a concern. This stage involves formulation and stating of the problem, perhaps in the form of a question. At this stage it can be very helpful to envisage 'how things will be' if the professional concern is alleviated or the problem is solved. This process can help in the evaluation of the action research. Has the desired outcome of the change been achieved?

2   Planning the change involves the development of a solution to the problem. A thorough exploration of the issues at this stage is crucial in order fully to understand the true nature of the issue. Care though is important at this stage to ensure that the 'right' problem is being tackled.

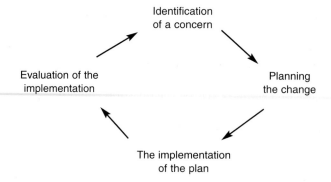

Figure 3.1 The main stages of an action research cycle

3 Implementation of the plan. In this stage the solution to the problem is put into operation.
4 Evaluation of the solution. It can be helpful to implement the *actual* outcomes of the implementation against the outcomes that were *intended* at the outset.
5 Further modification of practice in the light of the evaluation.

In addition to these important stages, the crucial aspect of the process is the continual cycle of action and reflection that must take place if the participants are to learn and develop as professionals during the process.

There can be considerable benefits from action research for organisational change. They include the following.

1 Action research engages the individual in the process. This individual engagement enables first-hand learning about the experience of change and what it means.
2 Action research following the model outlined in Figure 3.1 includes an evaluation component which can help to ascertain the value of the change.
3 Important additional outcomes of action research can be an increased ability to reflect on experience and an enhanced capacity to change. The development of these capabilities is an important leadership task, as we discuss in Chapter 9.
4 Involvement in the action research and intervention processes can add significantly to an individual's personal theories of their educational and management practice and the improvement of practice.

Frameworks and guidelines for managing change

In this section we explore various frameworks for understanding change and guidelines for successful change management.

Fullan's staged model

Michael Fullan (1991) identifies a series of stages in the management of educational change. They are as follows.

The initiation stage   Important positive influences in this starting phase are:

* the existence of quality innovations on which the change innovators can draw
* access of schools to innovations
* advocacy from central administration
* teacher advocacy of particular innovations
* the impact of external change agents
* the absence or presence of community pressure

- new national policies and the funds available to support them
- the willingness of schools to see the possible wider benefits of any particular innovation.

Implementation   Fullan lists key factors affecting implementation as follows.

- *The characteristics of change.* The need, clarity, complexity, quality and practicality of the change will all impact on the implementation.
- *Local characteristics.* The context, at various levels – regional, community, headteacher/principal and teacher – will influence the implementation.
- *External factors.* Factors outside the institution, such as central and local government and other agencies, will have an effect on the implementation.

Continuation   For an innovation to continue and become institutionalised depends on whether:

- the change becomes embedded in the structure of the institution
- there is a critical mass of staff at a variety of levels who are skilled in the new ways and are committed to them
- there are resources to provide some form of aftercare to support the initiative and to help develop those new to the innovation.

The strength of Fullan's work is that he explores the full complexity of change, and considers the stages at all levels from individual teachers to central government. In this way, he helpfully addresses the issue of the multiple perspectives on change. The model though still has a linear and staged feel to it. In practice the implementation of change is not like that. Also, it is concerned with the change episode or event as opposed to the ongoing, continual change experienced by many educational institutions.

The Everard and Morris systematic approach

Everard and Morris (1985) offer what they refer to as a systematic approach to change. It involves six stages as follows.

A preliminary diagnosis or reconnaissance   This investigation stage requires a balanced assessment of the implications of the proposed change, its magnitude, the level of support for the proposed change, its feasibility, and the context for change including the other planned changes that may be happening simultaneously and the organisational climate.

Determining the future   In this stage, the future scenario of the organisation is described. If the change is substantial this should be a wide-ranging review focusing in particular on the context.

Characterising the present   This stage involves describing the present in terms of the future. It is a question of describing where the organisation is now in relation to where it wants to be in the future. Everard and Morris suggest that this process involves a detailed consideration of the stance, expectation, demands and influence of the various stakeholders inside and outside the organisation.

Organising the transition from the present to the future   Everard and Morris suggest that the management of change requires a style and structure very different from that of the status quo. Failure to provide this different style and structure is a frequent cause of unsuccessful implementation. It has to be said that the creation of change groups to manage change in educational settings is a luxury that many schools would struggle to afford. Very often the same people manage the implementation of change and the maintenance of existing organisational activity.

Drawing up plans   This stage involves the following:

- the detailed specification of all the activities that relate to the overall purpose of the change
- specifying activities and tasks
- making target dates clear
- indicating any linkages between activities in the overall change process
- ensuring that the plan is cost effective in terms of time and resources
- monitoring and evaluation.

Evaluating the change   Monitoring and evaluation are important for two reasons. First, there is a tendency for systems to regress. Monitoring and evaluation will help to find out the extent to which the change is becoming embedded and will help to institutionalise the change. Second, by judging the gap between intention and outcome the value of a change can be ascertained.

Again the value of this model is that it provides a secure framework for action. However, Everard and Morris's model suffers the same problems as Fullan's staged model (to which it bears some similarities), that change is seen as rational and linear. Everard and Morris are sensitive to this weakness and suggest that the model should not be used inflexibly and without careful thought.

The unfreezing–moving–refreezing model

The unfreezing–moving–refreezing model of change, which was first set out by Kurt Lewin, sees the management of change in three stages: unfreezing the present, moving to a new situation, and refreezing. The detail of these different stages is as follows.

Unfreezing the present   This unfreezing process involves a trigger of some kind that illustrates the inadequacy of the present and initiates a press for change. There is then a process that confronts and/or re-educates the institution and those in it. A number of actions can promote the unfreezing. These include:

- using data to point to the inadequacy of current practice
- engaging change agents (either external consultants or new appointments)
- creating a sense of crisis which enhances the sense that the current practice will no longer do.

Moving to a new situation   This stage involves a move to the new, desired situation. Those participating in the change will probably require support during this stage.

Re-freezing   In this part of the change process, the changes set in place in the moving stage become part of the institutional practice. This part is essential to avoid regression to the state that existed before the change process began.

Lewin's model is a very helpful framework. It has a shape and a natural logic to it. But it does have some limitations, which include the following.

- It focuses thinking about change on to consideration of time-limited episodes of one-dimensional change.
- Any organisational change, as has been outlined previously, is always multiple change. In almost any institution, a change in one part will have knock-on effects in other parts. Indeed, there is a case for arguing that any change must have additional effects elsewhere in the organisation in order for the change to be accommodated.
- Any change sets in motion other changes that were unforeseen at the start of the process. Part of the difficulty of managing change is that it is very difficult to foresee what will happen once the process has been started. This difficulty can create further problems in setting boundaries around the changes that have been triggered.
- Finally, as Kanter, Stein and Jick (1992) point out, organisations are not ice-cubes and change is much more complex than Lewin's formula would have one believe. They argue that the organisations are never frozen even at the outset but are fluid entities. Also, the overlap of the stages, and the overlaying and interpenetration of other changes, hide the extent to which Lewin's stages are in fact discrete and identifiable phases.

Kanter, Stein and Jick's criticism draws attention to a further criticism of Lewin's model, that of the nature of the re-frozen state. Lewin's model would indicate that re-freezing creates another static and fixed state. This permanent and stationary position may not be the case. Indeed to 're-fix' organisational processes may not be desirable in a modern institution where the environment is changing rapidly and where there is a continual pressure to improve.

Some guidelines for managing change

One difficulty with putting into action any model for the implementation of change is that those initiating the change are left with the problem of deciding exactly what actions to take. The contexts and content of change are so varied that it can be difficult to know what to do, or where to start. In response to this difficulty, a number of writers offer suggestions or guidelines for the managers and leaders of organisational change. Yukl (1994) usefully summarises these guidelines under the headings of developing a vision for change; political/organisational actions during implementation; and people-oriented actions during implementation.

Guidelines for developing a vision for change   The development of a vision for change features very strongly in the leadership literature. It appears to be central in setting the destination of change, that is, some kind of representation of the objective or the target of the change process. Vision also appears to be valued in terms of determining the direction of the organisational change. Guidelines for creating a vision are as follows.

- The vision should be a simple and idealistic picture of a desirable future.
- The vision should not set out detailed steps, quantitative targets or milestones.
- It should emphasise the ideological benefits rather than the immediate tangible gains.
- The vision should be attainable and not a fantasy.
- It should be grounded in the current reality as far as can be ascertained.
- Any vision for an institution should address assumptions about what is important to that institution, how the institution should relate to the environment, and how people who work in and with the institution should be handled.
- The vision should be focused enough to guide strategy, but should also be flexible enough to allow scope for enterprise and creativity in strategic action.

Yukl identifies the following principles that should underpin the development of a vision for change.

- *Involve key stakeholders in the process.* Any change will require the support of key stakeholders. They will need to own the change, and their views may be helpful in refining the vision.
- *Identify strategic objectives that have broad appeal.* An exploration of

objectives will help to clarify values and ideals. Shared values can provide a strong foundation on which to base the change.

- *Identify relevant elements in the old ideology.* Even if radical change is required, identifying elements of the existing values and ways of working that should be retained may help the change process.
- *Link to the core competences of the institution.* If the institution has the capability to bring about the change, then the vision will be more credible. It is important therefore to link the vision to the central capabilities of the institution.
- *Continually assess and refine the vision.* It is important that the creation of the vision is not seen as a passing phase or fad that is then forgotten as the organisation goes about its 'business as usual'. The vision needs to be kept alive by continual reappraisal and renewal if necessary. This process will involve a considered evaluation of the credibility of the vision. It will also entail continually drawing attention to the vision and what the organisation is attempting to achieve.

Guidelines for political/organisational actions during implementation
Yukl outlines the following principles that can help to guide political/organisational actions during implementation.

- *Determine who can oppose or facilitate change.* This principle is important in the planning of any significant change. Time needs to be set aside to work with all parties in the change process.
- *Build a broad coalition of support for the change.* The task of implementing substantial change is a major task (as we explore later in the book) and will need broad support.
- *Fill key positions with competent change agents.* Those in key positions in the institution must be committed to the change. If they are not, the progress of the change will be slow, difficult and may be blocked altogether.
- *Use task forces to guide implementation.* If the change is substantial, using project teams to work on the change can help to facilitate the change process.
- *Make dramatic, symbolic changes.* Significant changes that illustrate and symbolise the change can have a substantial effect on the way in which the change is perceived.
- *If necessary implement change initially on a small scale.* Making a change in one part of the system can provide tangible evidence of the feasibility of a change and its benefits.
- *Change relevant aspects of the organisational structure.* Frequently, a major organisational change requires a change in the structure of the institution. (But note, this suggestion is not to be confused with a typical management error of re-structuring *instead* of implementing change.)

- *Monitor the progress of change.* Monitoring is important for a variety of reasons. It enables:

  - unforeseen difficulties to be dealt with
  - learning from the change to be optimised
  - the different aspects of the change to be co-ordinated
  - information about the effects on all aspects of the organisation to be collected.

Guidelines for people-oriented actions during implementation   Again drawing on the work of leading writers in the field, Yukl provides a very helpful set of guidelines for people-oriented leadership actions during a change implementation.

- *Generate a sense of urgency about the need for change.* As a change progresses the perception of the need for it can fade. Creating a sense of urgency can energise those participating in the change and help to reassert the need for the change.
- *Prepare people to adjust to the proposed change.* Even if the change is beneficial and the need for it widely accepted in the organisation, those participating will still need to be prepared for it. The most important preparation work will have to be done on the emotional dimensions of change.
- *Help people cope with the emotional pain of change.* Because so many of our responses to change are emotional, the change process can cause real pain. The sense of loss, even a feeling of bereavement at the loss of the 'old ways', can be very powerful.
- *Tell people about the progress of the change.* Telling people what is happening can help to maintain commitment to the change, especially if work on the change process is going on behind the scenes. It can also help to reduce anxieties that may be the result of fantasies created by not knowing what is going on.
- *Show continued commitment to the change at all stages.* An essential task for the leaders of change is to continually express their commitment to it.
- *Empower people to implement the change.* Change that is imposed on the organisation only from the top is less likely to be successful than change that is driven from all parts of the organisation. Empowering members of the organisation to implement the change is a way of releasing energy from within the organisation.

The benefit of all these guidelines and the points they contain is that they provide a helpful checklist of prompts for those managing change. Also, they are at a level of detail that can guide specific action. But the difficulty with such checklists is typically their length. The problem for change managers is how to hold all the various points in mind as they steer their institutions through the minefield that is complex change. One way of keeping the main messages of such lists in mind, and also making sense of them, is to remember that all these points have a non-rational dimension. Managing this non-rational, emotional dimension is crucial in the leadership of change. Motivations for change – essentially the 'vision thing' – are largely non-rational and will have a powerful emotional basis. The politics of change will also be closely linked to emotions, especially anxiety. Emotions call up and mobilise powerful forces in individuals, groups and institutions. Emotions and politics are therefore closely intertwined. All of the guidelines for managing people during change have an emotional underpinning. They are primarily about managing the emotional responses of individuals and groups to change.

Frameworks for understanding change

The context–content–process model

The context–content–process framework for analysing change was developed by Andrew Pettigrew and his co-workers in an investigation of change in the National Health Service (Pettigrew, McKee and Ferlie 1988). They argued that most analyses of change were flawed because the analyses looked only at episodes in the change process. These snapshots were limited by time and appeared to have a clear start and finish. Pettigrew and his colleagues argued that organisational change was a process that occurred over time and in a context. This kind of change was very different from the analysis of one-off episodes and single events. The three dimensions of their framework are as follows.

The content in the context-content-process model refers to the particular focus or area under study. It is the 'What?' of change.

The context is divided into an inner context and an outer context. The inner context refers to the existing strategy, structure, culture, management and political processes of the institution, which will influence the process. The outer context is the wider, perhaps national, social, political and economic context, and the interpretation of local and national policies and events.

The process of change is the actions, reactions, responses and interactions of the various players who have a stake in the change. It is the 'When?', the 'Where?' and the 'Who?' of change. The process also embraces the particular influences that are currently at work.

During change, there is a continual interplay between the content, the context and the process. The process is very important. It is the mechanism by which changes are legitimised or delegitimised. The content of the change is ultimately a product of this legitimisation process.

The model is a very useful framework for the analysis of change. It can be argued that the model does not give sufficient emphasis to the *purpose* of the change, although an interpretation of the context can give insights into why the change is taking place, and the intention behind any particular change action. A full understanding of the purpose of change is essential. It can be crucial in helping to elucidate fully what is being changed, and can also give a deeper understanding of the process.

Revolutionary, incremental and continual change

Meyerson and Martin (1987) describe three different types of change: revolutionary, incremental and continual. Any particular change process may fit one of these models, or elements of it may be of one or more of these types.

- *Revolutionary change* is often organisation-wide and leader-centred. It may be initiated and driven by the single heroic leader. It is a high-risk strategy because if the change is deep and substantial there is a danger that it may run out of control.
- *Incremental change* is the term for a localised change process in which there are variations, adaptations, re-workings and experiments among and within the various sub-systems of the organisation. As such the changes tend to be isolated and disconnected. It is difficult to predict the implications of such changes for the change process overall.
- *Continual change* is where individuals undertake ongoing attempts to change and adapt. As a consequence there is a continuous change throughout the institution. The changes undertaken are likely to be issue-specific with individuals adjusting and altering their practice. This kind of change is relatively uncontrollable.

These different typologies can provide useful insights into change processes in organisations including schools. As with all models, they are useful heuristics through which we can learn about and understand change. In the schools we studied, elements of all these different kinds of change were visible. In the early stages of the improvement journey, revolutionary change appeared to dominate, with the widespread changes set in motion in danger of running out of control. In the later stages of the improvement journey incremental and continual change, arguably present even in the early stages, became predominant. As far as the applicability of Meyerson and Martin's model to educational change is concerned, a major factor which controls the changes is the strength of professional socialisation and the norming influence that such factors exert. These factors serve to limit the scope for change.

Metaphors of change

The conceptualisation of change is notoriously problematic. Notions of change and the sense we make of our experience of change may vary over time. Changes in institutions emerge over time, and our rationalisations about change reflect our experiences and our subjective interpretation of them. Wilson (1992) argues that the very idea of strategic change involves assumptions about the linearity of time that are questionable. Instead the interpretation of change is a *post hoc* rationalisation, often dependent on the outcome of power struggles, within and outside the organisation.

The journey metaphor is frequently used in the change literature to model the process of organisational change, and is well established in the educational change literature (Fullan 1993, Hopkins, West and Ainscow 1996). Models of educational change frequently have an underpinning movement/journey metaphor. For example, schools are referred to as 'moving' (that is, changing) or 'static' (not moving) or 'stuck' (not moving and incapable of doing so) (Hopkins, Ainscow and West 1994). It is a metaphor, we will use to provide a framework for making sense of the process of radical change in the schools we studied. The journey metaphor has a number of attractions.

- It conveys an impression of moving from one place to another, which in a sense accurately conveys what the schools were attempting to do. They did not wish to be in the position or the place they were in.
- It is not too narrow in scope. It is open to a wide range of interpretations and therefore can help to make sense of events and occurrences.
- It can embrace the non-rational dimensions, particularly the emotional dimension of change. Indeed many of the emotions associated with undertaking a journey, are similar to those experienced in organisational change.
- There is a time dimension to a journey as indeed there is to organisational change.

The disadvantage of the journey metaphor is that it can constrain thinking into a linear, staged view of change. It may also suggest that there is only one acceptable or proper route. In fact organisational change is rarely linear and staged, and there are many routes through the organisational change process.

Leadership

Leadership is surely one of the most problematic notions in managing and organising. There is no doubt that it is important; in fact its importance seems to be increasing. In education in Britain and elsewhere, leadership is being emphasised increasingly as a factor, if not the factor, that 'makes the difference'. It is seen as making the difference between schools that are performing adequately and improving, but slowly, and schools that are effective and performing well, and where change for improvement is easily handled. Somewhat paradoxically, as the importance and eminence of leadership have grown, understandings of leadership have declined. Leadership theories are enormously diverse and wide-ranging, covering for example decision making, charisma and strategic change, and yet all leadership theories seem incomplete. They never seem quite to grasp the essence of it. Leadership theories are frequently complicated, while in practice leadership looks so simple, effortless and straightforward. There is a sense in which leadership may have become a spent concept as a result of over-use and lack of definition. It is as though the notion is in danger of collapsing under its own weight, such is our psychological investment in it and our expectations of it. However, as stated earlier, it appears that leadership is one of the factors that make the difference. It may not be enough on its own, but it is certainly important in the management of change. That is, leadership is almost certainly necessary, but without other positive influences is probably insufficient to implement change for improvement in schools.

Frameworks for understanding leadership

However leadership is configured, there is a general acceptance that it is centrally concerned with the use of power to effect change. Schemas for understanding leadership are usually chronologically based. Attempts to understand leadership at the turn of the nineteenth century focused on 'great men' (sic), and their heroic nature and apparently unfathomable leadership ability. In the mid-twentieth century, the study of leadership moved to an examination of leadership traits and the personal attributes of leaders. This stage in leadership research was followed by the study of leader behaviour. This approach focused on what leaders actually do. A third era of leadership research focused on the power of leaders and the influence they exert.

All of these approaches to finding out the essence of leadership – that is, leaders as great men, leadership traits and the power and influence of leaders – are leader-centred. In contrast the situational approach predominant in the 1960s and 1970s focused on the context of leadership and the impact the context has on leadership action. The context covers a multitude of different factors, including those in the local situation in which leadership is enacted, and the wider policy and strategy constraints and opportunities. Importantly, the context for leadership includes the characteristics of those who might be led, the followers.

One outcome of this succession of different approaches has been to under-value the contribution and importance of the earlier ones. For example, only recently has there been a re-emergence of the significance and value of the 'heroic leader' and leadership charisma. There is a good case for arguing that understandings of leadership traits and behaviours, the ways in which leaders influence, and the effect of the context, can all contribute to a fuller understanding. The problem is that these different themes in leadership research have all been overlaid, and together create a very complex and in many ways unhelpful picture.

Levels of leadership

Part of the complexity of leadership is that it can operate at different levels. These are the leadership of the self, of individual others, the leadership of groups, and the leadership of the whole institution.

Leadership of the self is long established in the leadership literature. Just as, according to the old adage, 'You can't manage others if you can't manage yourself', then 'You can't lead others if you can't lead yourself'. It would be almost impossible for a leader to communicate a mission and vision for the institution to the members of that institution with energy and enthusiasm without having a personal vision and mission. For individual leaders, self-leadership involves:

- identifying personal objectives and accomplishing them
- understanding and holding to personal priorities
- being reflective about but not dwelling on their leadership behaviour
- understanding their leadership role, purposes and boundaries.

Leadership of individual others is so obviously important that it is somewhat surprising that the distinctive impact of leaders upon individual followers was ignored in early research into leadership. The interrelation of leaders and individual followers, the so-called dyadic approach, covers two main themes.

- *Leader–member exchange* explores how the leader develops individual and separate leadership–follower relationships, within which the two parties mutually define the role of the follower. Different individuals may establish very different exchange relationships. Early research explored how these individualised relationships created an in-group and an out-group. Later work made it clear that effective leaders had meaningful individual relationships with all parties, not just those who were members of a particularly favoured 'in-group'.
- *Attribution theory* is largely concerned with the processes by which a leader determines the reasons for a follower's effective or ineffective performance. Attribution theory also embraces what the leader then decides to do about it.

Leadership of small groups and teams hinges on the factors that determine their performance. A greater awareness of these factors enables the leadership to be more effective. The key factors include the following.

- *The commitment of the group members to the task:* the greater the commitment the better the group performance.
- *The ability of the members of the group* will impact on task performance, particularly when the group task is complex.
- *The clarity of the roles of individual members* is important particularly if the task is complex, multi-dimensional and has potential for unpredictability.
- *The overall strategy of the group in performing the task* is obviously important in group and team performance. The leader has a significant role in designing and shaping that overall strategy.
- *Co-operation and teamwork* is essential especially if member–member contact is close and extended. Leaders have a role in ensuring effective teamwork and co-operation.
- *Resources* are essential for group/team performance. The leader has a key role in managing the boundary of the system (see Chapter 4) in order to ensure that the group has sufficient resources to complete the task.
- *External co-ordination* is important if the group is dependent on other groups and teams for the completion of its own task. The integration of the group's activities with those of other groups is a key leadership task.
- *Leadership* in self-managed groups and teams is likely to be shared and exchanged in a dynamic way according to the needs of the group in relation to its primary task. It is not likely that effective leadership authority will be consistently vested permanently in one individual.

Leadership of institutions is perhaps the most obvious way in which we view leadership. It is taken as read that all institutions need an *ex officio* leader. The common-sense view is that leaders are essential and have an impact on the performance of the institution. A number of writers, however, pose an opposite view, arguing that performance depends on factors beyond the leader's control. A leader's scope for manoeuvre in a mature organisation will always be restricted. Also, there is a good case for arguing that people exaggerate the importance of leaders and leadership in order to defend themselves from (and make sense of) the paradoxical and contradictory nature of complex organisational events. Many writers argue that it is not the power of individual leaders that makes the difference, but their ability to make and maintain political coalitions.

Explorations of leadership have tended to centre on only one level, while arguably to be effective the individual leader has to operate at all levels. Further, although monitoring the environment features in the leadership literature, the notion of the leadership of an institution's environment is relatively under-explored. This point is significant in education, where relations with key groups in the institution's environment, such as parents and the wider community, are crucial.

Leadership versus management

The distinction between leadership and management remains the subject of continuing debate. While no one appears to argue that the two are the same or even equivalent, the degree of overlap between leadership and management is a matter of contention. The overlap is understandable since the two forms of action are so broadly conceptualised. For Yukl (1994) 'it is obvious that a person can be a leader without being a manager and that a person can be a manager without leading'. Other authors, including for example Rost (1998), assert that it is possible to both lead and manage simultaneously, and that there is little point in arguing otherwise. An important issue is that distinguishing between leading and managing is a matter of characterising processes, not people. Simplistic distinctions may serve only to stereotype and downgrade insensitively the work of many for whom the term 'manager' is their occupational title. This point is significant in the context of education, where the rise of leadership as a way of organising in schools seems to be at the expense of the status of management and administration.

Distinctions between managing and leading rest on a number of factors and interpretations. Leadership is viewed as being concerned with change, influence, relationships, people, strategy, inspiring and motivating and the creation of meaning. Managing on the other hand is concerned with stasis, authority (usually hierarchical), ensuring correct operations, controlling, monitoring and problem-solving. Rost (1991) clearly distinguishes between management and leadership while not denigrating management. Rost differentiates leadership and management in four domains.

1   The nature of the relationship. Leadership is a non-coercive, multi-directional, influence-based relationship. Management however is an authority-based relationship, where authority is uni-directional and regularly and systematically coercive.
2   The terms 'leader' and 'follower' are not the same as 'manager' and 'subordinate' respectively.
3   Rost is clear that 'leaders and followers intend real changes whereas managers and subordinates produce and sell goods and/or services' (Rost 1991: 112).
4   Rost also comments that the changes intended or enacted by leaders and followers reflect their mutual purposes, whereas the production of goods/services is the result of the co-ordinated activities of the managers and subordinates.

Transactional leadership and transformational leadership

The leadership literature distinguishes two forms of leadership: transactional and transformational. Transactional leadership, which results in a

lower order of improvement, is the result of a leader–follower ex‹
process: a transaction. The leader meets the followers' needs if
mance measures up to their 'contracts' with the leader. The no‗
transformational leadership, which was initially characterised by Burns
(1978), has been refined by numerous others. Transformational leadership brings about a higher order of improvement. The transformational
leader raises the level of awareness of the significance of outcomes and
processes, getting the followers to transcend their own self-interests for
the sake of the team and importantly raising the need level or expanding
the range of needs in the followers. Bass (1990) has subsequently clarified
transformational behaviours as the 'four I's':

- *idealised* influence as charismatic behaviour, which arouses strong
  emotions in the followers and identification with the leader
- *individualised* consideration, which includes giving support, encouragement and motivation to followers
- *inspirational* motivation, which entails communicating an appealing
  vision, modelling the right kind of behaviour, and using symbols to
  focus the efforts of followers
- *intellectual* stimulation, which is behaviour that increases awareness of
  problems and persuades followers to view problems from a new
  perspective.

The four key behaviours clearly have an educational/learning emphasis.
As such they may be considered highly appropriate as the basis for leadership models in educational settings. Further, transformational
leadership appears to motivate followers to adopt a critical reflective
approach to practice, to actively engage in a consideration of their work,
and to experiment with ways, perhaps radical and creative, of improving
the processes and outcomes. These functions resemble experiential
learning processes and promote reflective practice. Also, they are
consistent with the notion of leader as 'learning guide' which is implicit
in many contemporary views of organisational leadership.

The limitations of leadership ideologies

Leadership ideologies, that is, particular sets of leadership ideas, approaches
and strategies, consistently applied, are inevitably, ultimately flawed.
Consultative and autocratic styles, shared leadership approaches and participative styles are all undone by the situational and contextualised nature
of appropriate leadership. Further, the contingent nature of leadership
action is likely to be exacerbated by leadership's primary purpose, which is
to bring about change in the context. Thus, leadership ideology and action
must continually be re-configured in response to the change that leadership
has itself brought about. Further, leadership action is always provisional. It

is temporary, conditional and likely to be subject to later alteration. Good leadership is, somewhat paradoxically, uncertain in nature.

Metaphorical imaging and leadership

Understandings of leadership are complicated by the fact that the term 'leadership' seems to lend itself to metaphorical imaging and therefore to diverse interpretation. In the literature, leaders are variously described as 'heroes', 'visionaries', 'liberators', 'stewards', and 'tenants – of time and context'. While the use of these metaphors may result from the complexity of leadership as a concept, it may also indicate that leadership is largely concerned with the non-rational, emotional and even spiritual aspects of organisational life. Although there is some consideration of the interplay of leadership, emotions and the influence of the unconscious in the literature, the interrelationship remains relatively under-explored. Arguably, there is scope for a much more detailed exploration in this area.

Leadership: a single or social influence?

Although visions of leaders are typically of the single heroic figure, many assert that in complex work organisations, the position of the single, heroic leader is untenable and ultimately unsustainable. Many authors argue that shared responsibility for leadership functions and the empowerment of subordinates is more likely to be effective. In practice, leadership is frequently experienced as a reciprocal process embedded in social systems, where influence is cycled recursively among the players in the system. Although this perspective on leadership is relatively under-researched, such group-relations approaches offer considerable promise for understanding leadership in institutions, especially educational ones.

School effectiveness and improvement

The pressure of 'new public management' on schools, especially the obligation to manage their performance, is causing them increasingly to focus on ways of improving pupil achievement. By definition this notion of improvement implies change. Change is involved in the process of becoming effective if individuals, teams or institutions were not effective in the past. Change is required if individuals, teams or institutions are to become *more* effective and to improve the ways in which they complete their tasks.

This section briefly reviews some of the relevant issues in school effectiveness and improvement. It first explores the nature of effectiveness and describes some of what is known about the characteristics of effective schools. The section then considers the nature of school improvement and how the process of improvement is often portrayed.

What is school effectiveness?

There is now a considerable body of evidence to indicate that different schools impact differently on pupil achievement. Although that impact may not be as great as might be hoped, some schools are more effective at enabling pupils to achieve than others. Although there is no widely accepted common definition of school effectiveness, in general schools considered to be effective are those in which pupil progress is greater than might be expected. Attempts at definition usually refer in some way to the notion of adding value to the pupil's starting capability. Definitions also typically include some notion of comparison with other schools.

Characteristics of effective schools

A review of the international school effectiveness literature undertaken by Sammons, Hillman and Mortimore in 1995 found that although approaches to education vary from one country to another, successful schools have distinctive features in common. The eleven key features identified are listed in Table 3.1 (page 40).

Stoll and Fink (1996), also describe how a task force, established by the Halton Effective Schools Project, developed a model which grouped together many of these characteristics into three broad categories.

- *A common mission:* a shared and communicated vision of school goals and priorities. The principal plays a major role in the encouragement of teachers', parents' and pupils' involvement in, commitment to and responsibility for the vision.
- *An emphasis on learning:* characterised by teachers who have and convey high expectations to their students. Teachers also use a variety of teaching and monitoring strategies, and work together to create curriculum materials linked to the school goals.
- *A climate conducive to learning:* where morale and self concept are high, due to active involvement and responsibility on the part of students, recognition and incentives, and fairness and consistency with regard to student behaviour. The learning environment is attractive, with work displays and attention paid to comfort. It is also inviting to parents and members of the community, who are also involved in school life.

(Stoll and Fink 1996: 16)

Although the eleven features listed by Sammons, Hillman and Mortimore appear of equal value, in practice some are of greater significance than others. This view is clearly expressed by MacGilchrist, Myers and Reed

Table 3.1 Key features of successful schools

Professional leadership	Firm and purposeful A participative approach The leading professional
Shared vision and goals	Unity of purpose Consistency of practice Collegiality and collaboration
A learning environment	An orderly atmosphere An attractive working environment
Concentration on teaching and learning	Maximisation of learning time Academic emphasis Focus on achievement
High expectations	High expectations all round Communicating expectations Providing intellectual challenge
Positive reinforcement	Clear and fair discipline Feedback
Monitoring progress	Monitoring pupil performance Evaluating school performance
Pupil rights and responsibilities	High pupil self-esteem Positions of responsibility Control of work
Purposeful teaching	Efficient organisation Clarity of purpose Structured lessons Adaptive practice
A learning organisation	School-based staff development (supplemented by attendance at appropriate external training courses)
Home-school partnership	Parental involvement

Source: Sammons, Hillman and Mortimore 1995

(1997), who argue that there are three essential core characteristics of an effective school, which if present can help to create the right conditions to enable schools to become effective institutions in terms of their pupils' progress and outcomes. These characteristics are as follows.

1   High quality professional leadership and management.
2   A focus on teaching and pupil learning.
3   The development of a learning culture within the organisation, where the school staff are willing to be learners and to participate in a staff development programme.

*The educational change process: the school improvement
journey*

The research literature is very helpful in pointing to the factors that may
make a school effective. It is however perhaps less helpful in giving insights
into the journey which represents the improvement/change process and in
indicating how to enable that process to take place. As discussed earlier in
this chapter, the journey metaphor is often used in discussions about the
development of organisations. It is used in the school improvement literature where it captures the 'dynamic element of the improving school'
(Hopkins, Ainscow and West 1994). Fullan (1991) shows how the change
process unfolds over a period of time. Fullan also describes change in
educational organisations as a 'journey, not a blueprint. It is non-linear,
loaded with uncertainty, and sometimes perverse' (Fullan 1993). He goes
on to argue that change is complex, and that until you start the journey you
do not know what is going to happen.

The journey metaphor has been used to good effect to describe schools
that are at different stages on the journey. Rosenholtz (1989) describes a
model that classifies schools as 'moving' or stuck'. Hopkins, Ainscow and
West (1994) expand the model to include four types of school.

1 *'Stuck'* schools which are often failing schools.
2 *'Wandering'* schools which, although changing, have little focus or
   clear vision of the way forward.
3 *'Promenading'* schools which are complacent, and are reluctant to
   change.
4 *'Moving'* schools are 'active' schools and have achieved a healthy
   balance between development and maintenance.

In developing the model further, Stoll and Fink (1996) identify five
types of school. Their model is useful, as individual schools can use it to
identify into which category they fall and devise appropriate improvement
strategies. Three of their categories are failing schools, that is those that
are 'cruising', 'struggling', or 'sinking'. 'Strolling' schools are neither
particularly effective nor ineffective; they are considered to be 'very
average schools'. 'Moving schools' are those which are moving forward
and becoming more effective. They know where they are going, and have
systems and the motivation and capability to get there. They know what
needs to be improved and how to implement appropriate strategies to
ensure success.

What is meant by school improvement?

A very widely accepted definition of school improvement emanates from
the OECD sponsored International School Improvement Project (ISIP),

where van Velzen and co-workers incorporated research findings into a comprehensive statement:

> A systematic, sustained effort aimed at a change in learning conditions and other related internal conditions in one or more schools, with the ultimate aim of accomplishing educational goals more effectively.
>
> (Van Velzen *et al.* 1988: 48)

The University of London Institute of Education School Improvement Network's *Bulletin – Research Matters* (1994) gives a detailed and very useful breakdown of this widely accepted definition of school improvement. It very helpfully sets out the different dimensions of the school improvement approach.

Systematic: School improvement needs to be carefully planned and managed and usually involves changes in school organisation in order that it can be built into daily activity. Monitoring and evaluation are also essential.

Sustained: Successfully implemented changes will not usually serve their purpose unless the initial drive behind them continues. Sustained change is a process and depends on innovations being built into the structure, until they are part of the school's natural behaviour, not just in terms of school policy, budget or staffing but also through procedures to pass innovations on to those who will be involved in the future. Persistence is a critical attribute of successful change.

Effort: Change not only requires the co-operation and commitment of staff but also their willingness to recognise that internal turbulence is a healthy sign of genuine engagement with the initial problem. As every person views change subjectively, there is a great potential for conflict. But no one says that school improvement will be easy: smooth initial implementation is usually a sign of trivial change. Significant changes to the status quo will inevitably require initial sacrifices of time and careful management of what may be emotional responses to increases in uncertainty.

Change: Not all change is improvement but all improvement is change. Looking at the wealth of international research, a common theme is of change giving the appearance that something substantial is happening when it is not. In all stages of the change process – identification of need, initiation, implementation, institutionali- sation and continuation – people involved must recognise the need for change, be committed to the particular improvement focus and feel that they have ownership of it, for the change to have any meaning.

Learning conditions: Real school improvement may involve a series of changes or multiple innovations. Although the school may have a specific focus for its endeavours, the conditions that support learning must also be a focus for change.

Other related internal conditions: Successful school improvement is not restricted to teaching-learning activities but extends to supporting roles, relationships and structures. These need to be directly addressed. Perhaps most importantly, school improvement strategies usually fail if they do not directly address the distinctive culture or ethos that is to be found in each school, which profoundly affects pupil motivation and achievement.

In one or more schools: Improvement must take place in the school since to be successful there must be a mutual adaptation of both the specific focus for change and the teachers, whose professional lives are often substantially altered by it. The school is also located in an educational system where there are great benefits to be reaped through collaboration and co-operation with other schools and through support from local authorities, universities or external consultants.

Ultimate aim of accomplishing educational goals more effectively: The ultimate aim of school improvement is to achieve a range of goals that will enhance learning, achievement and development amongst pupils.
(Institute of Education 1994: 1–2)

The ultimate aim of school improvement is therefore to enhance pupil progress, achievement and development. For Stoll and Fink (1996) a school which is well placed to achieve sustained improvement is one that has the following characteristics.

1 It enhances pupil outcomes.
2 There is a clear focus on the key tasks of learning and teaching.
3 The school builds its capacity to manage change.
4 The school sets and limits its own direction.
5 It continually appraises its current culture.
6 The school works to develop positive cultural norms.
7 The school has a strategy in place to achieve its goals.
8 It attends to the internal conditions that enhance change.
9 The school is able to maintain the momentum of improvement even when conditions are not favourable.
10 There is monitoring and evaluation of processes, progress and achievements.

Chapters 5, 6, 7, and 8 illustrate the improvement processes that were implemented by the schools in our study. The research evidence from our study will not provide instant recipes and solutions. We hope, however, that our findings will stimulate discussion within schools as they work to tackle their existing priorities for change. It would be a mistake to seek simple solutions for problems which are often very complex. Knowing what has contributed to making these schools more effective does not necessarily provide a guaranteed blueprint for improving every school. It is important to recognise the self-evident truth that each school is unique. Every school operates within its own context and has its own problems and opportunities. Also, all definitions of school improvement highlight the fact that improvement strategies must be well planned and managed over a relatively long period. If schools are to become more effective, they must not only be aware of the characteristics of effective schools, but also focus their efforts on systematically enhancing their own ability to manage change and sustain the impetus for change.

Modelling radical educational change for improvement

A model of educational transformation

From the findings of our research, the nature of the radical educational change can be modelled in the educational transformation grid illustrated in Figure 3.2. This model is based on those that have been developed by Rosenholtz (1989), Hopkins, Ainscow and West (1994) and Stoll and Fink (1996). In essence, in these institutions the purpose of the change was to become both effective and changing/improving, as the figure illustrates. Some of the schools we studied came from a position where they were both static and with a very low capacity to change, and they were ineffective in adding value to the pupils' starting capability. Because of the enormity of the change required of them, and the very different culture and practices in a school which has undergone that change, the process of change is appropriately termed 'educational transformation'.

A number of considerations arise from this model.

1   This transformation can apply to 'educational systems' at a number of levels, from an individual teacher to a department or team within the school, to the whole school. It could also apply to key stakeholders in the school's environment, and arguably it should do so.
2   It could be argued that moving from ineffectiveness to effectiveness is a transactional change in that it is relatively straightforward and contractual in nature. However, in educational settings particularly, the move to effectiveness is never simple because of the very high levels of emotion, especially anxiety, associated with the tasks of teaching and learning.
3   Moving from a static position to a changing one is arguably a transformational change. It requires a qualitatively different approach to the tasks of teaching and managing. The tasks and the teaching role become dynamic, complex and in themselves capable of change and development.

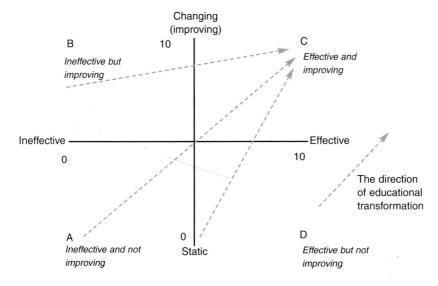

Figure 3.2   A model of educational transformation

4   The complexity of the educational process, the perpetual consideration of the focus of effectiveness, and the process of improvement through reflective practice in reality mean that measures of effectiveness and improvement on the scales in the diagram are continually being reset. That is, the 10/10 position can never be achieved. What is point 10 in the scale today may be point 8 on the scale tomorrow.

5   In education, the change from say A to C on the diagram has a moral purpose and represents 'good' change because of what the new position means in terms of the educational opportunities offered to the pupils and students.

6   Although effectiveness and improvement are represented on separate axes in this diagram, they are interrelated, if only because the purpose of the change is both to ensure effectiveness in present practice and to ensure effectiveness in the methods and systems of improvement at all levels.

7   As we explore in Chapter 9, this grid has very important implications for the purpose of leadership in school improvement.

Concluding comments

This chapter has explored some of the key issues in educational change and in organisational change in general. It started with a section that considered in a speculative way why change in schools is so complex. There followed a section that looked at some of the perspectives on the management of change. Next there was a section on leadership. The final section has briefly explored the notions of change in educational settings, and in particular has addressed the issues of school effectiveness improvement. Underpinning all of the issues that have been reviewed is the emotional nature of organising and changing. The acts that create organisations and change organisations have an emotional component and generate emotional responses (even though these may not be visible). These emotional components and responses become woven into the organisational fabric, and over time become what we experience as organisational culture. The next chapter explores some of the implications of this emotional interweaving in the taken-for-granted emotional life of organisations. It also considers some ways in which we can make some sense of and manage the emotional dimension.

4 The institutional transformation perspective

Introduction

At the end of the preceding chapter, we confirmed that the emotional content of organising is one of the reasons why effective organisational change is so difficult. This chapter explores that idea further, but importantly, we also add another dimension: social systems theory. This additional dimension is important because it gives a framework for working with the emotional component of organising. Without that framework, those charged with organising effectively may be left stranded: 'You've shown me the problem. What do I do for the best?' The interplay and conflict between emotion, our conscious and unconscious defences against emotions and external reality, and a systemic view of organising, all potentially give some ways for considering 'what to do for the best'. This linkage of the emotional processes – the psychodynamics – and systemic thinking is called institutional transformation.

This chapter explores and explains the idea of institutional transformation. The ideas contained in this chapter come from numerous sources. Important ones are French and Vince (1999), Gabriel (1999), Hirschhorn (1997), and Obholzer and Zagier Roberts (1994). Following a preliminary examination of the notion of institutional transformation, there is a section that briefly explores psychodynamic theory. The following section then briefly examines social systems theory. The final section considers some significant related issues such as leadership, power and stress. This final section also provides an explanation why schools in particular are locales for high levels of emotion.

What is institutional transformation?

Institutional transformation contains a number of interlinking themes which can be grouped under the headings of psychodynamics and social systems theory. It is a very useful set of ideas which help to:

- explain the behaviour of institutions and the people who work in them

- give a rationale for the most appropriate institutional behaviour
- manage institutional change.

Psychodynamics is the study of mental processes and forces. It is concerned with interplay, conflict and tensions between these forces, and the way in which they collide and clash with our desires and the external reality. One of its purposes is to understand and explain the non-rational behaviour of individuals and organisations. Non-rational behaviour is significantly influenced by the unconscious. The unconscious is the part of our minds that is the repository of all kinds of unknown thoughts and feelings which have accumulated throughout our lives. These unconscious processes influence our everyday thoughts and actions, although they remain hidden. As a result of this influence, apparently rational acts by members of an institution can have unconscious and non-rational origins. The same is true of the rules, routines and rituals – the culture – of any institution.

The unconscious has an effect on the behaviours we use to protect ourselves against the pain associated with difficult emotions such as sadness, sorrow and anxiety. These protective behaviours are known as social defences, and they take on various forms. The purpose of social defences is to separate the individual from reality, and they can be very resistant to change. Using psychodynamic theory to explore social defences and to understand the reasons for them is interesting, but on its own may not be helpful. It may reveal the problem without attempting to provide a solution. It is at this point that social systems theory comes in. Social systems theory is a very potent way of exploring and structuring the processes, roles, tasks, and interrelationships of individuals and institutions. The linking of psychodynamic theory and social systems theory is very important. The two approaches complement each other. On its own, psychodynamic theory can help to reveal, diagnose and explain organisational events and processes. Social systems theory, again on its own, may only provide a 'thin', one-dimensional and technical view of the individual and the institution. Linking the two together provides a very powerful instrument that can help to explain organisational phenomena, provide a rationale for understanding change, and help leaders and change managers bring about radical institutional change. This is the reason for the use of the term 'institutional transformation'.

Aspects of psychodynamic theory

The importance of the unconscious

Sigmund Freud was the first person to draw attention to the idea that not all our thoughts and feelings are consciously accessible to us. He argued that many of those inaccessible ideas and emotions, particularly difficult ones, are not known to us and remain locked away in the unconscious part of our minds. They are hidden in the unconscious as a form of censorship or defence because of the distress and anxiety they would cause if they were known. Although, by definition, we are not consciously aware of these ideas and emotions, they have a significant influence on our conscious thoughts, feelings and behaviours.

Freud first proposed the idea of the unconscious at the turn of the twentieth century. Since that time, his work and the precise nature of the unconscious and its formation have been critiqued and developed by numerous other psychoanalytical psychologists such as Carl Gustav Jung and Melanie Klein. However, the central concept remains. The unconscious is an influence on our conscious behaviour, and the notion of 'the unconscious' can be helpful in explaining why actions that have surface rationality and validity may at the same time have an unconscious and hidden meaning. It is particularly useful when thinking about people's behaviour in work institutions and the ways in which those institutions operate.

Freud used the image of an iceberg to describe the relationship between the conscious and the unconscious parts of the mind. The conscious is the part that shows above the surface. It is there for us to be aware of when we are awake, and for others to know. Freud estimated that our conscious mind occupies only about a seventh of the total. The unconscious, which occupies the remaining six-sevenths of our minds, contains notions that are completely hidden from us. By definition we are not aware of them. The unconscious contains our secret hopes, fears, desires, anxieties, urges and terrors. We can never gain direct access to the unconscious. The value of the unconscious to us is that it is the place where past disturbances and traumas can be kept safely. Locating these thoughts and feelings in such a place is necessary for our survival. By putting these notions away, we can get on with our lives without being explicitly troubled by them. However, the unconscious does influence behaviour in what Freud termed 'derivatives'. He argued that ideas from the unconscious seek expression, and they achieve this by linking with thoughts that are innocuous and acceptable. In this way they are allowed to reach consciousness.

At the boundary between the conscious and the unconscious is the preconscious. This 'layer' occasionally reveals clues about the thoughts and feelings that have been consigned to the unconscious through slips of the tongue called parapraxes. These are the so-called 'Freudian slips'.

Freud used his theories to explore aspects of organisational life in the church and the army, but he did not pursue this avenue of enquiry other than in general terms in his later sociological works. There can be little doubt that the conscious actions of members of a work institution are influenced by their unconscious thoughts and feelings. It would be remarkable if they were not. So, just as in other settings, people's behaviours at work and institutional processes that people create and sustain, may have a surface rationality and validity. At the same time their behaviour may simultaneously have unconscious and hidden purposes. A considerable body of literature on psychoanalytic conceptions of organisational behaviour has developed since Freud's early work. (A very small selection is included in the annotated bibliography at the end of this book.) However, for a variety of reasons, using psychodynamic theories to explore and explain organisational life is still in its infancy in relative terms. It is particularly under-developed in our understanding of schools. This lack of development is all the more surprising given the nature of the work of schools, and the fact that they are particular locales for emotion and anxiety. There is a good case for arguing that it is in these very settings that the influence of the unconscious is at its greatest.

Defence against emotional pain

In addition to pointing out the significance of the unconscious, Freud also drew attention to the ways in which we try to protect ourselves against the pain associated with unpleasant and difficult emotions. These protective patterns of behaviour are called social defences. They may have been learned over a long period, and their origins perhaps date back to the earliest stages of an individual's or institution's life. Social defences are important because of the way they protect us against the pain linked with strong feelings.

Arguably, anxiety is the dominant difficult emotion, in itself and because of its link with other emotions. For example, a person may be anxious about experiencing other unpleasant feelings such as sadness, sorrow and dismay. There may also be anxiety associated with pleasurable feelings. What price might one have to pay subsequently for feeling good now? Anxiety can also drive the generation and expression of feelings. At least by having feelings of any kind one knows one is alive and safe from an empty and apparently meaningless existence. So anxiety and emotion are inextricably intertwined, with anxiety having a central and crucial place.

Some social defences are useful but some obstruct change. They also block contact with reality. This role as a defence against reality is arguably their key purpose and value to the individual – and the institution. Also, because of their important purpose and the fact that they do their job very effectively, they are often repeated in response to new anxiety-laden situations. They become part of the scripts on which individuals and institutions base their lives. Also, and very importantly, social defences can be very resistant to change. There is a case for arguing that the more anxiety-laden an institution, the more it is likely to resort to social defences. According to writers on psychodynamic phenomena such as Kets de Vries, Miller and Hirschhorn, these social defences include the following.

Resistance This social defence is the maintenance of the status quo by opposing any change. In this way, the anxiety associated with the change is reduced. Importantly, resistance also reduces the anxiety associated with revealing that a response to the proposed change is essentially emotional and not rational. For example, in schools there could be resistance by some teachers to a statutorily enforced curriculum change on the grounds that it is an unwarranted intrusion by central government into their professional responsibilities. This resistance may be a defence against the anxieties of having to teach unfamiliar subject material.

Repression When recollections, urges and feelings are too anxiety-provoking they are assigned to the unconscious by a process known as repression. For example, the professionally and personally unacceptable feelings that teachers may have towards their students may be repressed in order to give protection from the anxiety that such feelings provoke.

Regression When events at work carry a great deal of emotion and/or anxiety individuals may resort to behaviours that have been learned earlier in their lives in order to limit the pain associated with those feelings. These behaviours will include those learned in the earliest stages of a person's life, and therefore may be very child-like.

Covert coalitions As a way of coping with the emotions of working, members of an institution may have recourse to familiar relationships that have protected them from anxiety and emotional pain in the past. This defence can be viewed as a particular form of regression. To gain relief, individuals regress to the kinds of relationship in which they and the colluding other or others are well versed. These relationships may be parent–sibling relationships where the quasi-parents and siblings gain protection by the re-enactment of these kinds of role. They act as containers of anxiety. An example of a covert coalition in education is a father–daughter relationship acted out between an older, experienced male headteacher and a younger, newly-qualified female teacher. The benefits for the teacher could be security and the avoidance of criticism by a figure in managerial authority. The headteacher might benefit by the relationship enhancing his capability to achieve compliance, and because it removed any dangerous sexual dimension. Another example is brotherly or sisterly relationships between a group of heads of department, say, between the heads of the science subject departments in a secondary school's science faculty.

Identification Individuals may seek to limit the anxiety associated with enacting their own behaviours by identifying with others. In a school, heads of department may seek to identify with the headteacher in order to gain protection from the anxiety associated with their managerial work. For this reason and others (see Chapter 8), all leaders have to 're-create the new', that is, to change and adapt regularly and frequently. In this way, followers do not become limited and restricted in the expression of their full potential by what is, in effect, the object of their envy.

Reaction formation   Occasionally, individuals will gain protection from the complexity of organisational life by the process of reaction formation. Working life is full of contradictions and unresolvable paradoxes. These can cause an inner tension and anxiety. Protection from this anxiety is gained by over-emphasising one of a pair of contradictory characteristics rather than holding them in balance. For example, a headteacher may find it hard to hold in mind that all his staff have both valuable and not so valuable qualities, and seek to idealise the behaviour of some at the expense of others. These others are consigned to the not-favoured category.

Denial   The process of rejecting and putting aside any unacceptable aspect of the external reality is termed 'denial'. These aspects may be thoughts, feelings and emotions which are too difficult to cope with, largely because they are too anxiety-provoking. They are pushed out of conscious awareness and into the unconscious. For example, a teacher in a primary school may deny that a forthcoming inspection is likely to be a cause of anxiety and real concern. Denial may on occasion be confirmed through negation. In negation, an individual may persistently and repeatedly reject a particular idea when that idea does not need to be disavowed so overtly. The teacher anxious about inspection may consistently assert that there's really nothing to worry about, and that the impact of inspection is always over-estimated.

Organisational rituals   The term 'ritual' is used to describe an established procedure or aspect of practice that has no apparent connection to a rational understanding of experience. These reified practices are probably the most durable and externalised form of defence against work-related anxiety. For individuals in a work institution, including teachers, these rituals can give structure, security and a sense of order to a potentially unstructured, insecure and chaotic working life.

Splitting and projection   A very common protection against anxiety and emotion is a process whereby difficult feelings that give rise to internal conflicts are split into their differentiated elements. The process of splitting is often accompanied by projection, where difficult elements are located in other individuals and objects rather than in the individual. This condition of splitting and projection is known as the paranoid-schizoid position. The alternative to the paranoid-schizoid stance is the integrated position. With this approach, which is called the depressive position, the individual gives up the security and simplicity achieved through splitting and projection, and faces the confusion, paradox, inconsistency, incongruity and conflict created by the mismatch between internal and external realities. An example of splitting and projection is a teacher with low self-esteem who, because he cannot bear any of his own feelings of inadequacy, separates them and projects them onto others. This projection of negative feelings could be achieved by continually moaning about his head of department who he insists should do his job better. This process makes the head of department have the feeling of inadequacy, not the teacher. It is the only way the teacher can gain relief from the emotional pain of his own feelings of incompetence.

Other consequences of splitting include projective identification and counter-transference. Projective identification is an unconscious inter-personal interaction whereby the recipients of a projection react to it in such a way that their own feelings are affected. So, in the example outlined earlier, the teacher's negativity could have a serious effect on the confidence of the head of department. These states of mind created by projective iden-tification are known as counter-transference. How individuals and groups respond to these processes has important implications for the following organisational phenomena.

- *Role differentiation.* This refers to the clarity with which roles are defined. If roles are inadequately defined, they are more likely to be shaped by the projections of others, thus trapping individuals in a kind of psychic prison not of their own making.
- *Role suction.* This phenomenon refers to the process whereby, through projection and counter-transference, groups force a member into a much-needed role.
- *Scapegoating.* In this process, all the reasons, and of course difficult feelings associated with an institutional failure or inadequacy of some kind are projected on to on a hapless and possibly innocent but (perhaps unconsciously) willing recipient of such projections.

In a group setting, these projections and other anxieties have to be contained. This containment role is arguably the central one in organi-sations. It can be argued that anxiety containment is a role which teachers, leaders, mentors, trainers and even parents have in common. In addition, leaders must have the capacity to change lest they fall foul of such potentially entrapping projections that may constrain their lead-ership actions. These projections may limit the diversity and creativity of their leadership practices. These ideas, particularly the leader's role in the containment of anxiety in educational change, and the importance to leaders of maintaining the capacity for individuation and variety, are developed later in the book.

A central point in the consideration of all these social defences is that they can be acted out at a range of levels from the individual, through groups/teams/departments, to complete institutions, geographical regions and even whole nations.

Some instances of these phenomena in the school environment are now discussed.

Resistance   In Britain, the way in which many grammar schools resisted the introduction of comprehensive schools in the 1960s and 1970s is an example of institutional resistance. A non-rational purpose of this resistance could have been to protect themselves from the anxiety connected with teaching what were perceived to be difficult, less able pupils. The resistance could have been a defence against the distressing feelings associated with a perceived loss of esteem as a result of teaching in a comprehensive school rather than a grammar school, or having to teach different subjects and in a different way.

Repression   Teachers and schools may repress feelings associated with perceiving part of their role as 'providing workers to service the capitalist economy'. Interestingly, making explicit that purpose of schools and schooling is now very much out of favour. Such notions and the difficult emotions they call up are nowadays lost in a liberal rhetoric of providing young people with opportunities, a sense of achievement and empowerment.

Regression   For an educational institution, being part of an educational community will have an emotional dimension. The simultaneous benefits and difficulties brought about by participation in any group may cause anxiety. To cope with these difficulties, schools may adopt an excessively competitive stance, thus re-enacting the leader's earlier relationships. Alternatively, they may seek to form collaborative relationships with other schools nearby, again reflecting a predisposition to earlier (and successful) patterns of behaviour.

Covert coalitions   Schools may develop and act out relationships with other schools that are reminiscent of other powerful lifetime relationships. For example, there may be sibling rivalry between a town's two comprehensive schools. Secondary schools may create a 'family' of 'feeder' primary schools.

Identification   Educational institutions may seek to identify with and emulate the practice or the ethos of other schools. This social defence gives protection from the perplexing feelings associated with the school becoming its own kind of school and attempting to meet the needs of its own stakeholders and communities. An example of this kind of behaviour is the way in which many comprehensive schools, in the early days of comprehensivisation, sought to emulate the ethos of grammar schools. The anxiety of moving to a new educational structure was assuaged with the slogan 'Grammar school education for all!'

Reaction formation Schools may seek to idealise particular parts of the institution, or key stakeholders, while unreasonably and consistently denigrating other parts or stakeholders. A school might cope with the difficulties of under-performance by blaming one department and idealising another: 'Our results would be fine if it wasn't for that wacky lot in the humanities department. Why can't all departments be like the science department?'

Denial Feelings associated with the under-performance of a school, for example, can be repressed and thereby ignored. The need for change is thus removed, and so is the anxiety that goes with it. Poor performance in the 'league tables' of GCSE results may be denied on the basis that such tables are meaningless or that 'You can't expect anything different with the kids we get'.

Organisational rituals Schools are awash with organisational rituals: uniform, prize day, reports, 'Miss' and 'Sir' and so on. Of course, all rituals bring real benefit, as do all social defences. They enter the history, mythology and folklore of schools. Arguably, however, they all serve to protect against difficult emotions.

Splitting and projection In institutions, functional and structural divisions can exacerbate splitting and projection. Dividing an institution into separate levels, divisions, departments and spheres of expertise may be essential for effective and efficient functioning. But such divisions are a very fertile ground for splitting, projection and self-idealisation. Subgroups may form and may be stereotyped by other groups. Potentially productive contact with other groups may be avoided to preserve self-idealisation based on these projections. These disorders can interfere with the tasks that require co-operative working. Ensuring the balance between differentiation and integration is crucially important. Of course schools, especially secondary schools with their various sub-groupings of 'years' and departments, are ripe for such splitting and projection.

Individual biographies

Past experiences, events, and relationships have an impact on all of us. They will therefore be an important influence on the behaviour of individuals in work organisations. These biographical influences can be particularly important when individuals have senior roles and play a prominent part in establishing the cultural norms of an organisation. The earliest stages in a person's life are usually the most important in an individual's growth and development. Psychoanalytical theories of personality formation suggest that the ability to tolerate uncertainty and anxiety (an important leadership characteristic) is largely based on emotional development during these times.

During infancy, there is usually a transition from a reliance on the primitive defence of the paranoid schizoid position to the higher order depressive position. In order to cope with feelings of both love and hate, primarily for its mother, the infant splits up good and bad feelings. In this way, there are only good feelings for the person the infant relies upon and its survival is assured. The bad feelings are projected elsewhere into bad objects outside her/himself, hence generating paranoid anxiety. With the consistent love of the idealised 'good enough' mother, the infant is enabled to move to the depressive position and to cope with ambiguous feelings and uncertainty. We continue to move in and out of these paranoid-schizoid and depressive positions during our lives. However, the capacity to remain in the depressive position is a sign of maturity and is more likely to enable an individual to remain in touch with reality. This ability to tolerate uncertainty is a key underpinning of leadership ability, but that is not to say that a leader with paranoid-schizoid tendencies may not be appropriate in particular situations and/or for short periods of time. However over time, a life modality that maintains close contact with reality and is able to adapt and be flexible is likely to be more useful.

The self-esteem of individuals in work organisations is another key factor in their behaviour. Self-esteem indicates the extent to which an individual values her/himself. Infants who experience a lack of love, inconsistent love or rejection by their parents are less likely to develop an adequate sense of their own worth. As a consequence, they feel that they are not worthy of being loved, arguably the most basic of human needs. This inference is then generalised into a wider sense of being not worthy. Arguably, the giving of the unconditional love that the infant demands is not humanly possible: good enough loving and valuing is what is required. Of course, a feeling of low self-esteem can be very valuable. It can provoke ambition, with the success that is achieved proving that the individual is, after all, worthy. It can generate an ability and willingness to work hard to make up for a perceived inadequacy. Low self-esteem can create a desire to achieve perfection, because only perfection will give a sense of approval, thus compensating for a perceived lack of self worth. It can engender competitiveness, because winning shows that, after all, the person with low self-esteem is better than every one else and must therefore be worthy. There is of course a downside to low self-esteem. It can lead to:

- individuals incorrectly gauging their ability, estimating it either too high or too low
- a lack of resilience

- stubbornness
- an unwillingness to take risks
- a lack of or fragile self-confidence
- an inability to cope sensibly with setbacks
- an unwillingness to assert needs and desires.

These factors – splitting and projection and low self-esteem – are not rational, and are deeply embedded. As a consequence, changing them can be very difficult. There is a view that low self-esteem is not 'curable' in the accepted sense. It can only be known, understood and worked with. An excessive predisposition to splitting and projection can be worked with, but the pathway is a long one. These issues and all social defences have a significant and valuable upside. They have distinct advantages and the 'life-script' they create can be a successful one. So, for the individual attempting to change these behaviours, there is the anxiety that the benefit the defences provide will be lost. The risk is that there will be no real benefit from changing, and anyway changing may mean taking up behaviours that have been long eschewed and disdained. These new behaviours might include producing less than perfect work, being ready to let others take the lead, and not trying to control the world as a defence against uncertainty. An individual may have to recognise that the imagined 'enemies' out there may have some good sides, may be facing similar problems and may even be worth positive regard.

Group mentalities

Another theme in the psychodynamic approach to the study of institutions arises from the seminal work of Wilfrid Bion (Bion 1961). He studied groups and the way in which they worked. His work on groups, much of which has been developed substantially by others, is directly applicable to the processes of individuals, institutions and groups within them. As such, the ideas from group relations theory form an important link between the psychodynamic themes in this section and the social systems theory described later.

There are two main tendencies in the way in which groups work: the work group mentality and the basic assumption mentality.

The work group mentality

In this way of working, the group members focus on carrying out a specifiable task and assessing their effectiveness in doing it. This task is referred to as the primary task. Of course, the notion of the primary task may seem somewhat superficial and an over-simplification when the idea is transferred to other work-related settings. This is perhaps particularly the case in schools, where the purposes of education are apparently complex and have always been a matter of contention. However the notion of the primary task is a very useful learning device. Consideration of the primary task can be a very useful starting point and a focus for discussion on the purpose of any institution, including a school. Such consideration allows discussion of the nature and structuring of the varied and multiple activities of an organisation. (But beware: there is always the possibility that endless consideration of the primary task is in itself a social defence against undertaking it.)

In the context of group tendencies, there are three kinds of primary task. The categories enhance the primary task's potential as a heuristic device. The different categories are as follows.

1   *The normative primary task* is the defined, formal or official task of the institution. The completion of the normative primary task enables the institution to achieve its aims, as defined typically by the institution's stakeholders. For schools, the normative primary task is the education of the pupils/students. Schools may well wish to encompass other tasks, such as the care and welfare of the pupils. While these other tasks are valuable, if they are pursued with disproportionate energy and resources they may detract from the achievement of the primary task.

2   *The existential primary task* is the task that the members of the institutions believe they are carrying out. It is the meaning and interpretation they give to their roles and activities within the institution. Again, for schools, this is the education of the pupils/students; but again, all too easily, energies may be diverted into apparently meaningful tasks which in fact do not contribute to the normative primary task. For example, a school may, quite rightly, view record keeping as very important. In practice, though, the time spent on the task may be excessive and have little impact on the quality of learning.

3   *The phenomenal primary task* is the task that can be inferred from people's behaviour. Their behaviour may be under unconscious influences and therefore hidden from the individual or group. Again, for a teacher, the primary task may be to enable mathematical learning in the pupils in her class. Unknowingly however, she may become preoccupied with other issues such as keeping strict order, or over-emphasising neat presentation of sums at the expense of ensuring the pupils have a grasp of number. Alternatively, a teacher may be unduly concerned with getting on with the pupils, but fail to make educational relationships that provide a basis for learning.

The basic assumption mentality

Groups working in this way have a propensity to avoid work on the primary task. Behaviour is directed at meeting the unconscious needs of the group members. A major need is the reduction of anxiety, and internal discord that may provoke anxiety in its own right. In the end, the perpetuation of the group becomes an end in itself.

Bion identified three kinds of basic assumption mentality: dependency, fight/flight, and pairing.

1 The *basic assumption dependency* mentality is where the group operates as if its primary task is solely to satisfy the needs and desires of its members. The group processes seek to ensure that the group members feel cared for and do not have to confront difficult issues, tackle problems or make significant binding decisions. Here, the focus on the normative primary task is lost. A group with this kind of basic assumption tendency would look to a leader to collude with this inactivity and to not face them with the problems. If the leader does collude, the group is likely to become dependent upon her/him. If the leader refuses, he/she may be viewed as harsh and uncaring. Clearly for the leader, there is a careful path to be trodden in moving the group from this tendency to a work-group tendency.

2 The *basic assumption fight/flight* mentality is where the group 'creates' some kind of enemy or danger which must be either attacked or fled from. To maintain this position, the danger must be present indefinitely. In groups with this tendency, there may be a culture of paranoia and aggressive competitiveness where the group is preoccupied by an external enemy. For example, in a school that has this tendency, staff meetings may be dominated by finding ways of upstaging a local 'rival' school (the 'enemy') as opposed to focusing on ways of improving performance of the primary task. In another scenario, meetings may degenerate into moaning about the lack of support and funding from the local education authority (another 'enemy'). This tendency is very effective at promoting a sense of togetherness and *esprit de corps*. For the group, it has the added benefit of preventing any work on the primary task and thereby avoiding the anxiety associated with it. The group may look to the leader to defend it against the enemy by organising action of some kind. Refusal to do this, and attempts to shift the group on to the primary task, may leave the leader open to charges of weakness and lack of courage. Again, the leader needs to be adroit in pursuing the right strategy and action.

3 In the *basic assumption pairing* mentality, whatever the actual problems and needs of the group, the group believes that a future event will save them. Salvation lies perhaps in a pairing or coupling between two members of the group, or between the leader and a person or object outside the group. The group may focus on the future as a defence against the difficulties (and anxieties) of the present and be motivated by a spurious optimism that things can and will get better. For the leader, bringing the group back down to the present is

likely to bring feelings of disillusion and disappointment. Once again the leadership strategy and actions need to be chosen carefully.

A number of issues arise from the notion of basic assumption tendencies. First, leaders can use the basic assumption mentalities to their advantage, and indeed skilful leaders do. Ultimately, however, the use of basic assumption mentalities to lead a group is inadequate on its own, and especially in the long term. It can only be a provisional strategy. In the end, for institutional success there must be a focus on the primary task. Also, understanding and managing the basic assumption tendencies of a school are very significant for a new incoming headteacher or principal. The correct diagnosis will enable the most appropriate leadership strategy to be put into place.

Second, group mentalities are very important in the management of change to improve educational achievement. As explained later in the book, enabling teachers and the school as a whole to focus on the primary task of enabling learning is itself a substantial task because of the particularly high levels of anxiety associated with teaching and learning. These anxiety levels increase if attempting to improve the way that the primary task is carried out is incorporated into the attainment of the primary task itself. Improvement implies change and change is always associated with anxiety. So teaching effectively while at the same time attempting to improve carries high levels of anxiety.

Third, all three basic assumption tendencies are social defences. They all reduce the anxiety associated with the group's normative primary task. If the leader is to make the group focus on the primary task, he/she has to contain the anxiety against which the basic assumption tendencies are a defence. This containment of anxiety is an important function for the leader in educational change.

Social systems theory

Thinking of organisations as systems can be very helpful. The term 'system' can of course conjure up all manner of negative images to do with repression, control and tyranny. These images are particularly at odds with educational processes and the work of schools. Despite that negative image, thinking in terms of systems can be very helpful in structuring and ordering management and leadership action. Systems thinking can give some clarity to the apparently unfathomable complexity of many work organisations including schools. In essence, systems theory is a simple idea, and it is this simplicity that makes it useful and gives it breadth of application. Systems theory can be used at the level of the individual, the group and the whole institution. Thinking in terms of systems – systems thinking – involves a creative use of systems theory, particularly open systems theory.

Open systems theory

The general idea of systems theory for organisations is derived from systems in living organisms. In essence, all living organisms survive by being open systems. Figure 4.1 is an illustration of an open system.

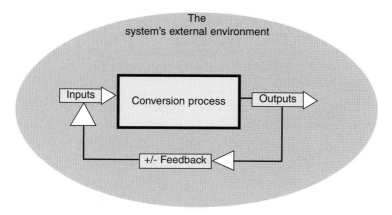

Figure 4.1 A diagrammatic illustration of an open system. The system's external environment surrounds the system.

In biological terms, the system model applies at the single cell level and at the level of groups of cells working together as organs, like the kidney and the liver. It also applies at the sub-system level of the whole organism, such as the nervous system or the digestive system, and at the whole organism level. Arguably, the open system model works at the group level too: for example the pride of lions or the flock of birds. At the whole organism, or even the sub-system, level there needs to be some kind of co-ordination. This system management is provided by superordinate systems that have a co-ordinating function. In the case of humans the main co-ordinating system is the brain, but of course the hormonal system provides an important co-ordinating function too. At all levels, the system has a selectively permeable boundary that surrounds and encloses the internal processes. All the systems and sub-systems require inputs and produce outputs.

The external boundary is a crucial requirement of an open system. It surrounds the internal milieu and separates it from the external environment. Without the boundary, the organism merges with its environment and ceases to exist as a separate entity. Boundary exchanges must be selective so that only designated materials enter and leave so the system must somehow manage movement across the boundary. The system requires various inputs to function effectively. The flow of inputs across the boundary and into the system is obviously crucial. The system also needs internal processes to do the work. Finally, if it is working properly, the system will produce outputs. These are the result of the conversion of the inputs by the internal processes. Again, these outputs need to cross the boundary and leave the system.

The parallels between systems in living organisms and systems in organisations are reasonably self-evident. Open systems theory has been used to great effect in understanding and designing work organisations, since the early work of Lewin in the 1940s in applying open systems theory to human systems in organisations. Lewin's early work has been elaborated subsequently, particularly during the 1950s and 1960s. In recent times, it has been superseded and overtaken in the contemporary organisational literature. This fall from favour may be due to the slightly mechanistic image of the notion of 'the system'. It may also be due to the emergence of other ways of thinking about organisations. Other images and metaphors have been used to describe organisations, and these have been especially useful in the postmodern era. While these other approaches are very helpful in explaining organisational events and processes, they are less useful in framing and structuring strategy and action. There has been a recent resurgence of interest in systems as a way of explaining organisations and framing action, especially in the context of the learning organisation. Open systems theory, especially when used creatively and simply, provides a valuable heuristic for the understanding of individual and institutional behaviour management and leadership actions.

The conversion process and role

The conversion process – performed by the internal processes of the system – is a representation of the role of the system. In a human system, the role is embodied in the expected pattern of behaviour associated with achieving the primary task of a particular system or sub-system. So teachers fulfilling their role display the patterns of behaviour commensurate with being members of the teaching staff of a school. This concept of role as behaviour associated with position in the system can be applied to other higher-level systems. For a department in a school, its role is exemplified by expected patterns of behaviour that are required of a sub-system, (in this case, the department) of the overall system (the school). For a school, it is the pattern of behaviour we would expect of an educational institution. Of course, in considering the notion of role, a number of questions immediately spring to mind. For example, what exactly is the role of the teacher? What behaviours do we expect of schools, and who is doing the expecting? Parents? Employers? Other schools? The point is that consideration of role is a very useful heuristic device, especially when considered in relation to the system's primary task.

Managing the boundary

In using systems theory to understand individual and organisational processes, boundary management is crucial. Controlling movement across the boundary is a central management and leadership task. Boundary management involves:

- being clear and definite about the primary task of the system
- managing the flow of information across the boundary into and out of the system
- making sure that the system has the resources required to perform its primary task
- monitoring the primary task so that it relates to the wider system and to the environment.

Boundary management operates at all levels: individual, group and whole institution. Individuals who are unable to manage their own boundaries cannot manage themselves. Individuals have to manage the boundary between their inner world – their needs, requirements, resources and assets – and their external reality in order to enact their role effectively. The boundary is therefore important in defining an individual's sense of self. For individual teachers, inappropriate boundary management might result in not being assertive in asking for what they want and need to do their job properly. In an inexperienced teacher, it might be exemplified in forming inappropriate relationships with pupils, say by being too friendly with them. In this case, there is no clear boundary between the teacher and the pupils. For experienced teachers, failure to manage the boundary may be apparent in allowing their skills to become out of date by not undertaking professional development activities of an appropriate kind. They have not managed the entry of resources into their own system to enable them to carry out their role effectively.

Managers who fail to manage the boundaries of the system for which they are responsible cannot manage or lead the system. For a head of department, effective boundary management might be ensuring that the department has adequate resources. It could also mean making sure that the members of the department receive information about wider developments in practice, and changes in policy, at school, local and national levels. Good boundary management might also mean managing the linkages with other departments in the school. For the headteacher, it might mean ensuring that the school is aware of new policy developments and that the school is meeting the needs of the institution's key stakeholders, such as parents, associate primary schools and higher education.

Boundary management requires a 'positioning' of management authority on the boundary. This maxim applies at all levels: the individual, the group, and the whole institution. At any and all levels, the manager who loses or gives up the boundary position, by being drawn into the system or by being cut off from it, cannot manage. The same applies to individuals within an organisation, in the way they manage their own boundary. At an individual level, leaving the boundary and joining the system can have significant consequences. It may result in an individual being too eager to satisfy the needs of others at his or her own expense. Failure to remain on the boundary and to manage the boundary can make an individual vulnerable to the unwanted projections of others. For the manager, it may mean joining the system for which s/he is responsible. Failure to delegate properly is an example of a manager joining the system. For a headteacher, it may mean joining the environment and spending too much time liaising with and working with external agencies at the school's expense.

The primary task

Defining the primary task of the system is important but also difficult. If the definition is too narrow or is in terms of the members' needs, the system's survival may be threatened. If it is too broad in terms of the members' resources, they will not know what to do for the best. None the less, consideration of the nature of the primary task can be very useful.

Problems associated with the primary task include: vague task definition; defining methods instead of aims; failing to solve conflict over priorities; and failing to relate the primary task to the changing environment. For any institution, focusing on the primary task is crucial, but the primary task in any group or work institution is always associated with anxiety. As we make clear in this text, the primary task of educational organisations, to enable learning, carries particularly high levels of anxiety. In education, there has always been debate and a lack of clarity about this primary task. While this debate may be appropriate, it can weaken this focus on the primary task, making the primary task more difficult to achieve.

Inadequate definition of the primary task creates problems with boundaries. If the task is not clear, boundaries come to serve defensive functions instead of helping to facilitate task performance. Members of the system are not sure what they are meant to do, so there is a temptation to preserve the 'turf' that they think is theirs, whether it is or not. As a result, boundaries may become impermeable or they may prevent productive interrelationships of sub-systems with each other and with the overall system.

Inadequate task definition may also permit task avoidance strategies. These strategies are seductive because they give respite from the anxieties associated with the primary task. If the task is not clear or carries too much anxiety, those responsible for it may retreat from the role boundary. The repertoire of behaviours associated with the role that might be used to achieve a clearly-defined task may well shrink. By focusing on the primary task, it is possible to develop what is called 'on-task leadership'. This also helps to avoid the abuse of power and to minimise basic assumption tendencies in the ways in which groups work.

The importance of feedback

According to the open systems model, the systems are controlled by what is termed 'feedback'. Control by feedback means that the output of the system is monitored in some way, and the level of the output is then used to influence the level of the inputs entering the system. Too much output, and the level of the inputs entering is reduced. Too little output, and the inputs entering the system are increased. This form of control is called negative feedback. The central heating and thermostat model is a useful example. When the temperature of the house is too high, the boiler is turned down. When the house is too cold, the gas entering the boiler is turned up. Of course the feedback can be used to influence the conversion process. If the weather becomes very cold, the central heating boiler can be turned up, or in extreme circumstances got rid of and replaced with a better one! Feedback can be positive too. In this case, an increase in the outputs can be used to increase the flow of gas into the boiler or to turn up the boiler. The room will get hotter and hotter. Unless it is controlled, positive feedback will push the system into overdrive.

The benefits and disadvantages of systems thinking

There are a number of benefits from using systems and systems thinking, some of which are now summarised.

• Systems thinking allows managers and leaders to focus on roles and functions rather than on people. It can also help them to see their role more clearly. It is very easy for individuals in organisations to become the role, rather than simply to be people who are taking up a role as part of the wider system. Thinking in terms of roles and functions can immediately reduce the anxiety associated with primary tasks. Those undertaking the role can completely fill the role right up to the system boundaries. They know what is required and what their responsibilities are. Importantly, they also know that they, as 'persons', are not 'the system'. This approach is particularly useful in the event of crises or mistakes. Peter Senge (1990) tells us that at these moments we must look at the system that allowed the event to occur, and how well the system dealt with it. When mistakes are made, it is not wise to point to the person; that approach simply generates a blame culture. Nor is it wise to focus on the event, because that reduces the opportunities for learning. Focusing on the event is only worth doing in order to learn from it and to improve the system that allowed the event to occur.
• Systems thinking reduces anxiety in the individual and in the institution, and therefore frees up energy to do real work. Paradoxically, although the primary task has anxiety associated with it, by focusing

energy and behaviour on the primary task, less anxiety is generated because there is less work on other non-productive tasks. Systems thinking can thus 'clean up' the individual's or the institution's work.

- Thinking systemically provides a useful lens through which to look at the institution as a whole. Exploring the various sub-systems and the way they inter-relate can give a clearer view of the institution. It can help to audit the work of the whole system and the various parts by looking at:

  - the resources the sub-systems need and have
  - how well the different boundaries are managed
  - the inputs and outputs of the different sub-systems
  - how the various sub-systems fulfil their roles
  - exactly how the sub-systems contribute to the outputs of the system as a whole.

- Systems thinking provides a very a useful framework upon which to base management action. This framework is particularly important in relation to boundary management. How well do individual managers manage their boundaries? Are they managing *on* the boundary? How do they manage the flow of information across the boundary? Systems thinking can also give insights into the whole management process. How well do individual managers fulfil their management role in taking responsibility for the system? How well are the processes and outputs of the system monitored? How are the resources that the system requires managed?

Some significant issues

Authority and hierarchy

Authority, differences in status and hierarchy are essential for the efficient functioning of institutions. They can be used to encourage effective working in others, and to create and implement new ideas and ways of working. They can help to cope with external threats and to take advantage of opportunities in the institution's environment. Hierarchical arrangements can also be useful in dealing with internal disagreements. Hierarchy and authority, by co-ordinating relations between the various parts of the system, can help define status and reduce conflict and competition. Authority within hierarchies can also allocate power, resources and status unequally. It is therefore open to abuse by those at or near the top, and there is no doubt that authority has within it the seeds of corruption and evil. The energies to which those high in the hierarchy and with authority have access, and the behaviours they can elicit in the followers (such as loyalty, discipline and self-sacrifice) have the capacity for both exceptional good and extreme evil. Authority is therefore extremely problematic.

One interpretation of authority is that it is the right to make a decision;

and in an institution, it refers to the right to make a decision that is binding on others. It is a role relationship between two actors within a social system where the actors are individuals, or larger sub-systems. Authority of one actor over another means that the first actor is entitled to make particular demands on the second, who is obliged to assent to them. In this interpretation, authority arises from an acceptance of the role relationship, or from the influencer's values that are grounded in identification and internalisation, not unadulterated power and subjugated compliance.

Authority has a number of sources.

From above, through a system of delegation   In a commercial institution which exists to make a financial profit, the managing director is responsible to the board of directors. In a public company, the board is then directly responsible to the shareholders and acquires its authority from them. The authority of the managing director then flows out, into and down the institution by means of delegation. In other kinds of institution which have different purposes, for example voluntary organisations, the hierarchy may be differently constructed. In educational institutions, such as schools, the authority is more complex. However, for the operation and strategy of single institutions, the governors are responsible to the local education authority. The governors then delegate their authority to the headteacher. That authority in ideal circumstances then flows out and into the school.

From below, through the members who willingly join an organisation
Arguably, those who willingly join a work organisation implicitly accept the structure and hierarchy of authority within the institution. In joining the institution, they hand some of their own authority and autonomy to those in authority, thus confirming the hierarchy of the institution they have joined. Without the sanctioning of authority from below, it is impossible to manage and lead.

From within the individual   This basis for authority is largely under the influence of an individual's relationship with figures in her/his inner world or past. A range of factors such as the individual's own self-esteem, the extent of her or his empowerment, her or his ability to cope with uncertainty, and her or his capacity to deal with conflict, will influence this authority in the mind. An important factor is the individual's 'self-inner talk'. These are the 'conversations' individuals may have in their own minds, and the messages from authority figures from their past.

It is important that those notionally in authority understand all the sources of their authority, from above, below and within. Arguably full authority is never attainable, and 'full enough authority' may be all that an individual manager or leader can achieve. In this way of operating, those in authority are continually reflecting upon and recognising their authority. At the same time, though, they also fully understand and work within its limitations. Such self-knowledge allows an individual to be authoritative as opposed to authoritarian. The authoritative state of mind parallels the depressive position (discussed earlier) where managers are in contact with the origins and ratification of their authority and with its limitations. On the other hand, an authoritarian approach can be likened to the paranoid-schizoid state of mind.

Responsibility

The essence of authority means being answerable or accountable for outcomes, either to a person in the institution or again in the individual's own mind. Having responsibility without the requisite authority and power to achieve outcomes can lead to high levels of anxiety which may result in stress. The link between anxiety and stress is discussed later in this chapter. Clarity of organisation structure helps to give clarity of authorisation and responsibility.

Power

Of all the different aspects of organisational life, power is possibly the most problematic. Bacharach and Lawler (1998) argue that power is a primitive term. It is too broad in scope, unrefined and therefore likely to be difficult to define. There is no doubt, however, that power is the key resource in organisational politics and is at the centre of all organisational processes.

In the literature, power in organisations generally refers to the ability of one person, the 'agent', to influence another, the 'target'. But that view is interpreted in different ways. Sometimes, it means the power differential, the 'net power'; sometimes it means the power that is available for use without unwanted consequences, the 'usable power'. Some writers consider that power represents 'potential', while influence is the actual use of power, 'enacted power'.

Historically, power has been conceptualised as the different kinds of power which agents have over others. Hardy's four dimensions of power (Hardy 1994) provide a broad and useful framework. The dimensions are as follows.

1   *Decision making:* the power to decide what decisions are 'on the agenda', and the power to make decisions.
2   *Non-decision making:* the power to suppress options and alternatives and to keep items off the agenda.
3   *Symbolic:* the power to shape peoples' perceptions to ensure that there is acceptance of the existing order of things.
4   *System:* the power that lies in the largely unconscious acceptance of the values, culture and structures of a system.

The first three forms are deliberate and conscious strategies by organisational actors to achieve their objectives. System power on the other hand works to the benefit and cost of individuals and groups without being explicitly mobilised.

Although power over others is apparently simple as a notion, in reality it is very complex. Sources of power and their legitimacy, dependency in relationships, and the sanctioning, salience and the unconscious experience of power all serve to complicate the issue. In recent times, the conception of power in organisations has shifted away from a model that sees it as being fixed and stable, where relationships are consistently configured on the basis of long-term power differentials. A more appropriate model, which conforms to the experience of many in organisations, is where power is experienced in relationships and in groups reciprocally and in a perpetually changing way. In these circuits, power is circulated recursively and multi-directionally as opposed to flowing consistently in one direction. This model provides alternative and perhaps more promising approaches to understanding some of the complexities of power.

As with power, the notion of influence is similarly contested. Established views of influence distinguish between three types.

1 *Instrumental compliance* is where the target of the influence carries out a requested action for the purpose of obtaining a reward or avoiding punishment, both of which are under the control of the influencer or agent.
2 *Internalisation* is when the target becomes committed to supporting and implementing proposals espoused by the agent because they appear to be intrinsically desirable and correct in relation to the target's values, beliefs and self-image.
3 *Identification* is a process in which the target imitates the agent's behaviour or adopts the same attitudes to please the agent and to be like her/him.

A person's sensation of perceived power and capability to influence, and/or powerlessness, is crucial. Individuals may project power outside themselves or they may be the recipients of projected power. The nature of those projections will determine whether that person is hated and feared or loved and admired. There is a very good case for arguing that just as power is cyclical and experienced reciprocally, so is influence.

Psychodynamics, systems theory and leadership

One of the most useful outcomes of the institutional transformation perspective is that it gives an insight into leadership. Leadership, certainly in Britain, is much in vogue in education at the present time. As we discussed in Chapter 3, there is a demand for it but at the same time understandings of leadership seem to be left wanting. Leadership as a concept remains slippery and elusive.

At a policy level, the rational, surface requirement for leadership has to do with the new ways in which public institutions are managed. This 'new public management' has in effect three dimensions. First, schools are separated into autonomous units with devolved responsibility for their own affairs including their finances. Second, schools are exposed to market forces and are expected to compete for pupils, which in the context of the present funding arrangements means money. Third, there is the performance management dimension whereby the performance of schools and the improvements in their performance are open to public scrutiny. All three dimensions put a premium on the leadership of schools. The increased autonomy emphasises the strategic leadership of individual schools. The impact of the market places a clear onus on the leader to steer the school to a secure niche in the market and to represent the institution in the market place. The management of a school's performance, and particularly its improvement, require the management of change, or in other words, leadership.

There are of course non-rational explanations for the rise in the value of leadership. The need for leadership may result from a feeling that leaders can satisfy un-articulated needs and desires. The expression of these needs may create enormous psychodynamic complexity. This interpretation could explain why leadership is in such demand at the individual, the group and the institutional levels. Leadership may simply be yet another social defence. In education, schools may be the unwitting recipients from society of the blame for (and anxiety associated with) society's ills. The splitting of this anxiety and its projection on to schools and teachers may be projected onwards to the leaders of schools through what Hirschhorn calls an 'anxiety chain'. 'There are things wrong with society': the anxiety. 'Schools are to blame': the projection. 'It's the headteachers' fault and if headteachers were better leaders, our anxieties would be reduced': the forwarding of the projection along the anxiety chain. Hence the perceived need for leadership in schools.

Leadership may be perceived as a preferable mode of organising because of its ability to contain anxiety. As argued earlier, the primary task of any work organisation has anxiety associated with it. Changes and improvements in the way the primary task is carried out also have anxiety associated with them. Arguably a key – if not the key – leadership task is to contain the high levels of anxiety associated with significant change. As we argue later in this chapter, schools are locales for particularly high levels of anxiety. Management, possibly with an image of being a rather cold, directive and technical approach to organising, may not be appealing as a way of organising in institutions where anxiety levels are high. Leadership as a person-centred, relationship-based activity has the capacity for containing anxiety, and may therefore be viewed as a more appropriate mode of organising than management in schools. It can be argued that the containment of anxiety is an aspect of any leadership or educational relationship: leading, teaching, mentoring, coaching, training, even parenting. The common task of anxiety containment links these activities.

Leadership may simply be a social defence against being managed. It may be an attractive way of subverting managerial authority and thereby defending against it. The rise of managerialism and the use of management authority in the public sector, including schools, has been the subject of much critique. The use of leadership ideologies with more appealing titles such as participative leadership, shared leadership and in schools, collaborative leadership and invitational leadership may be more acceptable than management with its coercive and manipulative connotations. As we discussed in Chapter 3, the relatively recent emphasis on collaboration in education may also act as a social defence against the anxiety associated with managing and being managed.

Leadership and narcissism, which is a tendency to exceptional self-admiration, are intimately connected. Elements of narcissism and the development of self-esteem and positive self-regard are crucial for human functioning. However, in excess, narcissism can be destabilising. Narcissism arises through insecurity and low self-esteem. The anxiety of low self-esteem, if unchecked, can result in a fixation on power and status and, in extreme cases, grandiosity and a sense of omnipotence. Narcissism can take two forms: constructive and reactive narcissism. Constructive narcissists are characterised by a predilection for introspection, a sense of positive vitality and a capacity for empathy. They can become excellent leaders. Reactive narcissists are preoccupied with a continual need to boost their deficient self-esteem, and are motivated by emotions such as envy, revenge and triumphalism. Reactive narcissism and the neurotic styles it generates are significant in defective leadership. However, reactive narcissists may overcome their feelings of bitterness and may then be motivated by reparation in an attempt to prevent others suffering as they have.

For both the leader and the led, there are benefits from the outcomes of narcissism. The followers may collude, albeit unconsciously, with the narcissistic tendencies that drive the strong leader. In this collusion, the leader has her/his narcissistic needs met by the adulation of the followers. The followers gain the protection from anxiety that the all-powerful leader provides.

Leadership may be attractive to leaders because it can legitimise the social defence of splitting and projection. It gives a separation from the anxieties of their organising role and responsibilities. Leadership may permit a licit separation from management, an activity that may be experienced as mundane, ordinary and merely 'operational' as opposed to the more grand 'strategic'. It may also sanction a separation from the even more workaday tasks and associated emotions of administration. By being the leader as opposed to the manager or the administrator, an individual avoids the difficult feelings associated with these tasks such as boredom, frustration and anxiety. Also, leadership with its largely future orientation may allow a separation from the emotions of the present. Finally, it is frequently asserted that leaders cannot be and indeed should not be 'one of the crowd'. Leaders can thus legitimately separate themselves from the 'rest' and the difficult emotions that close personal relationships with them might generate.

Schools as particular locales for anxiety

For a variety of reasons, schools have a number of features which means that they are locales for particularly high levels of emotion, especially anxiety.

1   *The special nature of the primary task of educational institutions.* The primary task of schools, enabling pupils to learn, carries anxiety, as do all primary tasks. However, it is a primary task centrally concerned with change. Anxiety is associated with almost any individual or institutional change, either as an instigator of change or a consequence of it. So the primary task of educational institutions carries additional anxiety.

2   *Learning is associated with risk and uncertainty.* Almost every aspect of learning – the desire to learn, the learning process or the outcomes of learning – is associated with risk and uncertainty. By definition, learning changes the learners, but there is always the risk that they will be changed in ways they cannot predict. Further, in schools, learning often takes place in judgmental and competitive environments. Successful learning and unsuccessful learning might impact on the self-esteem of both the learner and the teacher. A failure to learn may harm relationships with significant others, such as the learner's parents or teachers, who may have high expectations of the learner.

3   *The process of teaching.* Teaching is likely to be associated with anxiety. It is a complex and interconnected activity, and its many different facets have to be coped with at the same time. In the classroom, incidents both positive and negative have to be dealt with immediately. Classroom life is inherently unpredictable and is played out in a public arena. Potentially, what happens in a classroom on any one day may be talked about in literally hundreds of homes that evening. All of the classroom processes have a history, which may serve to confuse and complicate the present. For example, relationships between the pupils, relationship between the teacher and the pupils, and previous learning all play a part in what happens in the

classroom. All these characteristics are potential instigators of anxiety. In teaching, the teacher acts as a container of the anxiety associated with the learners' learning. This crucial role will exacerbate the teacher's sense of anxiety. Also, teachers may be the recipients of the projection by society of the troublesome feelings associated with any national failure, deficiency or decline.

4   *The nature of relationships in educational institutions.* Relationships in schools can invoke strong feelings and desires that can potentially cause anxiety. For example, there is a continual turnover of relationships in schools. There is the sense of loss as older pupils in whom so much has been invested leave the institution, perhaps never to be encountered again. New relationships have to be forged as younger pupils join the school. This turnover can cause considerable emotional turbulence which is not often acknowledged and is a potential cause of anxiety.

5   *New models of professional practice.* New understandings of professional practice, such as reflective practice, place responsibility on teachers to improve their practice through reflection on their actions. Such models of teaching can easily be viewed as deficit models of continuous improvement. These models can convey a message that teachers are to be condemned to a professional life of unending change driven by a fear that they will never be, and can never be, 'good enough'.

6   *Curriculum and management changes.* The level and extent of imposed change in recent years have increased levels of anxiety for teachers. Many of these changes have extended teachers' work into areas in which they may not have expertise. Curriculum changes have meant that teachers may have had to teach topics with which they are unfamiliar. They may have had to teach in different ways. Changes in the management of schools, for example local management and devolved budgets, have increased institutional separation, responsibility and accountability, all of which may have exacerbated anxiety.

7   *Changes in the external environment.* Recent changes in technology and in society generally have increased accountability in education and eroded the *ex officio* professional authority of teachers. The undervaluing of the teaching profession in Britain at least, and the requirement for schools and teachers to undergo external inspection, may have increased anxiety levels.

8   *The centrality of education.* Educational institutions are about the management of processes that are central to every person's life. In schools, these include maturation to adulthood, the preparation for adult life in its widest sense and the acquisition of qualifications that enable a pathway to lifetime success and security. As such, the work of schools is associated with powerful ambitions, motivations and aspirations. In this

work, the teacher is accountable not only to the child but to her/his parents and to the rest of society.

The fact that anxiety and emotion are central to the work of educational organisations is almost never explicitly asserted and remains hidden. The unspoken nature of anxiety and emotion has a number of implications, of which two are particularly important. First, the task of containing emotion and anxiety in educational organisations is embedded and thereby hidden or accepted in the taken-for-granted structures and processes of the institution. Second, for teachers to make explicit that coping with anxieties and emotions – their own and those of others – is a major determinant of their actions might seriously undermine the confidence of learners, colleagues and society in their professional competence and authority.

Stress and anxiety

The stressful nature of teaching is recognised almost as a matter of course. It is widely acknowledged and referred to in both the professional and academic literatures. However, the link between anxiety and stress is an interesting one. From the institutional transformation perspective, stress is the mental, physical and emotional consequence of institutional/societal anxiety being projected on to individuals, in this case teachers, who are ready, willing and in many cases very able to receive such projections. A major part of teachers' work is to handle such projections from their pupils. Educational managers and leaders also have a role in mediating the projections of institutional anxiety. So, in considering the emotional health of the institution, anxiety, the social defences against anxiety and the way anxiety and emotion are handled are the fundamental issues, not stress.

Concluding comments

This chapter has outlined some of the key features of a perspective on organising, which is known as institutional transformation. This perspective welds together the psychodynamics of behaviour in work organisations and social systems theory. Psychodynamic theory is very valuable in explaining the unconscious influences on behaviour. These unconscious influences provide an alternative explanation for apparently rational actions and also can explain non-rational and emotional behaviours in the management of change. The creative use of social systems theory, especially open systems theory, can provide a very helpful way of explaining and framing management actions. The key point is that these two main themes are inter-related, complementary and highly synergistic. They mutually add considerable value.

The use of the institutional transformation perspective is very appropriate for understanding organisational processes in schools. The psychodynamic perspective is very apt because of the high level of emotion and anxiety in schools. Schools are emotional arenas because of the special nature of their work. Social systems theory is very helpful because of the complexity of educational institutions. Systems theory allows a shape to be put on the practice of individuals, groups and whole institutions which otherwise can remain elusive. The institutional transformational perspective will be used to interpret the nature of the changes that have taken place in the schools involved in the Improving Schools Project. The accounts of the changes and this interpretation make up the following four chapters.

5 The challenge
The schools in the pre-acceleration stage

Introduction

Many of the schools in the study had made significant steps to change their in-school processes in order to bring about improvements in pupil achievement. For some, the starting conditions were a somewhat distant memory; for others their recollections of those times were all too close. From the data we collected, a number of challenges were common. Not all the schools had faced all the challenges, but many schools had faced more than one. That finding is not particularly surprising since many of the problems were linked or shared a root reason or explanation. Almost all the difficulties were however significant. It is therefore a tribute to the energy, commitment and professionalism of the teachers, the senior staff and the headteachers that they managed to move forward and overcome those challenges in the way they had.

This chapter briefly explores the main problems that the schools faced at the start of their improvement journeys. It also outlines some of the underpinning explanations of the challenges that they faced in attempting to bring about change.

The challenges

Some of the schools were in extreme difficulties at the start of their improvement journeys. One headteacher, typical of those who faced severe challenges, referred to his school as being on the 'verge of being labelled at risk'. Those we spoke to identified many problems. Typically, the problems related to a significant lack of focus on the core function of the schools: teaching and learning. The difficulties were also linked to the schools' 'internal conditions': the prevailing culture. Some of the schools had been ready to change and interestingly, resistance to change had not been universal. One headteacher was clear that: 'most staff were hungry for someone to give direction.' In a small number of schools the situation had been much more resistant. On occasions, the headteachers in such schools had to face strong opposition to proposed changes (see Chapter 6). In some schools, a mixed climate had prevailed. There had been pockets of resistance – sometimes fierce – in the midst of a climate in favour of change. This lack of uniformity had called for very high levels of contingent leadership action, that is, the capacity to vary the leadership action and style moment to moment, person to person, situation to situation.

In many of the schools, there was a trigger for change that was followed by some kind of early analysis of the difficulties the schools faced. We describe and explore these in Chapter 6. The following sections set out some of the specific challenges facing the schools as revealed by these early analyses.

An unsatisfactory environment for learning

In many instances, the physical environment of the schools had been unsatisfactory and did not support an atmosphere conducive to learning. The physical envirnment did very little for the morale and self-esteem of teachers and pupils alike. In many of the schools, scant attention had been given over the years to maintaining the buildings, many of which were old. The schools' grounds had been similarly neglected. The result was that in many instances, the overall environment had been bleak and unattractive. Many schools had significant defects to the fabric of the buildings, such as rotting window frames, leaking roofs, inadequate toilet facilities, limited storage space, outdated furniture and fittings, and poor decor.

The use of displays to promote and celebrate the achievements of the school and its pupils had been very limited or absent. Where pupils' work had been displayed, it was rarely changed. In many cases, standards of displayed work had been shoddy and showed little imagination, creativity or expertise. Such displayed work as there was made only a limited contribution to supporting teaching and learning.

In one school, the accommodation had been described in an external review as 'Drab and uninviting . . . . classrooms reflected the general squalor of the building. The general atmosphere was arid, uninspiring, showing little imagination, professional expertise or pride'. A parent described the accommodation in the same school at the time as 'Awful! The classrooms used to be awful. They were damp and there was always an unpleasant smell. A foul smell in the school.'

The newly appointed headteacher of another school had found that 'Classrooms were untidy with so much old furniture that children couldn't get around. The toilet situation for staff and pupils was horrendous. The whole set up needed an overhaul.'

In some of the secondary schools, specialist facilities for science, technology, physical education, music and art had been of poor quality and dispersed throughout the school rather than grouped together. Schools that were located on split sites had faced additional difficulties. In some instances, the split-site arrangement had created social divisions leading to an unproductive 'them' and 'us' attitude.

Inadequate resources

Some headteachers who had been new-to-post had found major deficiencies in equipment, materials and textbooks. This lack of adequate
resources affected the curriculum and limited pupils' access to high quality
material to support their learning. In these cases, there had been insufficient
textbooks and those that were available were outdated and rarely used by
staff or pupils. In many instances, teaching resources for specific areas of
the curriculum, for example mathematics and science, had been limited and
those that were available were not used effectively. In one school, resources
that were perfectly adequate and that could have been used to enhance
pupil learning had been locked away and rarely used. Often, school
libraries had been of poor quality.

Inadequate and ineffective management

Frequently, and perhaps unsurprisingly, there had been significant
problems with the management of the school. Typically, management
practice had been inadequate, as had been the structuring of responsibilities
and accountabilities. In some instances, management activity had been at
such a low level that there had been effectively no management presence.
Middle managers, that is, heads of department in secondary schools and
those with curriculum responsibility in primary schools, had generally
restricted their role. They had limited themselves to administrative tasks
rather than undertaking any role in the management of colleagues or acting
as the leading professional. In some of the schools, there had been no clear
management structure and roles and responsibilities had not been defined
clearly. Even where responsibilities had been well defined, the position of
staff with management duties was often untenable because their role was
not recognised. In the words of one such middle manager in a comprehensive school, heads of department had been unable to 'deliver the goods
because they had no non-contact time'. In some schools, those members of
staff in management positions were simply not carrying out their
management duties.

   This lack of capability appeared to have had a double effect. First, the
aspects of the school for which the members of staff were responsible
remained poorly managed. Second, these managers blocked the potential
contribution of those who had management capability and were ready to
exercise it. As one headteacher put it, 'the wrong people were in control'.
Some newly appointed headteachers had also found a widespread lack of
accountability. Those with management responsibility were not called to
account. In these instances, there was very little acknowledgement among
staff of a link between salary increments and the designation of responsibilities. In many cases, the history of change initiatives had not been good
and there was a record of change not being sustained and embedded.

Where improvement initiatives had been attempted in the past, they were often 'quick-fix' solutions that had failed to last.

Some newly appointed headteachers had had to deal with significant financial problems very soon after taking up their appointment. Sorting out these financial problems had been a crucial priority for them because it placed any future changes on a sound footing. Often the incoming head-teachers had not been given any forewarning of these financial problems. Typically, these financial difficulties were the result of staffing levels being too high, so the only way of rectifying the financial problems had been to reduce staffing levels. However, the resolution of these problems had often caused difficulties in the subsequent management of change as a teacher in one of the schools recalled:

> When the new headteacher came, the school was in a dire position financially. Before he came, the school had taken on extra members of staff. When he arrived, one of the first things he had to do was to get rid of some members of staff. It didn't go down well. It created a lot of bad feeling. . . . At times he was thought of as a 'hatchet man'.

A lack of collegiality among members of staff

The unsatisfactory climate of interaction between members of staff had been a characteristic of many of the schools at the start of their improvement journeys. During the data collection interviews, many respondents recalled staff working in relative isolation, behind the closed doors of their classrooms. This separation had meant that there was only limited contact with other colleagues and little exposure to new ideas and practices. The physical isolation of members of staff within schools, and the typical lack of a 'professional discourse' in schools, had also made it difficult for the staff to develop a common culture or shared language so that they could talk meaningfully about their teaching.

Frequently, staff had been only minimally involved in many important aspects of the school and had had little or no appreciation of whole school issues. As a result, there had been no cohesion for educational purpose and very little sharing of ideas or expertise on how the school might be run. In some instances, the staff did not appreciate the need to plan for the development of the school and for changes to improve pupil achievement. Members of staff had not seen the relevance of school development plans or planning. In some of the schools, when they had been asked to become involved the staff had not been able to understand why they were being included in the planning process. Many of the headteachers felt that the core functions of their school, teaching and learning, were not receiving sufficient attention at the start of the improvement journey. The monitoring of teaching and pupil performance had often been superficial. There had been little acknowledgement among the staff that low achievement had anything to do with what went on in the classroom.

Inadequate staff development

The poor management and leadership of the schools had often been reflected in the inadequate systems and processes for the development of the staff. Staff development had had little structure or sense of purpose, and typically there had been no written policy. In many of the schools, in parallel with inadequate management structures, there had been no formal allocation of specific responsibility for planning and evaluation of professional development activities. Little, if any, attention had been given to addressing the specific development needs of the school or the continuing professional and personal development needs of individual members of staff. In these instances, many of the staff had needed to have their knowledge and expertise updated. Staff development had generally involved one-off attendance at training courses, and focused on National Curriculum subject areas. In some cases, there had been resistance to professional development, with some staff viewing it as unnecessary. In the words of one headteacher, there was a prevalent attitude of 'We've been doing it this way for twenty years and we know what to do. Why are we being asked to do this?'

Not unexpectedly, there had often been insufficient follow-up after members of staff attended courses, and very little dissemination to colleagues in school of any new information or insights gained. As a result, the impact of staff development activities on classroom practice had been minimal.

Poor achievement, low expectations and insufficient attention to teaching and learning

According to a number of respondents, the location of the school and the history and culture of the area had had a significant impact on educational expectations and achievement. In many schools, the achievements of the pupils, measured for example by external examination results, had been well below local and/or national levels.

The low levels of achievement had generally reflected the limited expectations of staff, pupils and parents. Indeed, staff had often been content with their pupils' performance. In such cases, ineffective planning had often resulted in lessons that had insufficient challenge. Classroom activities were poorly organised and not well matched to the abilities or interests of the pupils. The monitoring of pupils' progress to support learning and to determine the extent to which pupils knew and understood what they were being taught, had been inconsistent. As a result, many pupils had under-performed. One headteacher, reflecting on the situation when he was appointed, stated that:

> The need for change was clearly indicated by the school performance tables which showed that the pupils' achievements had declined in the previous few years. While there was a perceived need for change, many staff wondered if in fact change could be brought about. There was a large measure of staff scepticism that we could raise standards of achievement. Poor achievements in external examinations were very much accepted as the status quo. The attitude of staff was that we cannot do this (improve) because these are valleys children.

Low expectations among teaching staff had also been apparent among the schools that were performing at higher levels. A newly appointed head-teacher had found that: 'There was a contentment that we were performing at that level. It was comfortable.'

Difficulties in implementing the National Curriculum

At the start of the school improvement journey, some schools had had difficulty in meeting the requirements of the National Curriculum. Where this had been the case, the problem had needed to be addressed urgently in order to ensure that the school fulfilled its obligations. An early inspection report of one of the schools we studied had identified major shortcomings in the staff's knowledge and understanding of the National Curriculum. One headteacher, describing the outcome of a curriculum review of her school, said that the review had found that:

> We weren't delivering a number of areas of the National Curriculum properly. We had to put together a completely new curriculum for September; new organisation, new timetable. We have had to rebalance the curriculum which gives a framework so that staff can deliver the National Curriculum in their subject areas.

When one new special school headteacher had been appointed, the curriculum had still been based on caring for the pupils and developing skills. There had been only limited attention paid to the delivery of a subject-based curriculum. The National Curriculum was just beginning to be implemented and members of staff were only at the early stages of inves-tigating how it might be modified for use in the school. Indeed, many staff had felt that the National Curriculum had little relevance for pupils with severe learning difficulties. The pupil care/skills-based curriculum was firmly in place, and to introduce the National Curriculum had therefore required not only major changes to school structures and systems, but also the substantial retraining of staff.

Unsatisfactory relationships between members of staff and low staff morale

In a small number of the schools we studied, the newly appointed head-teachers had found that relationships among the staff were far from harmonious. In some cases, a number of staff had clearly showed little commitment to the school's aims and the school's educational purpose in their day to day practice. Members of staff were often suspicious of new initiatives and there had been a lack of trust and openness between the headteacher and staff. These unsatisfactory interpersonal relationships had done little to foster productive working relationships. There had been little team spirit or cohesion among the staff, who were rarely involved in decision making. This deficiency had often resulted in a distinct lack of coherence and consistency in how the school operated. Reflecting on this period, one headteacher later indicated that: 'The atmosphere in the school was very unhappy . . . poisonous in fact. In the past, things were often handled very badly and staff constantly felt threatened and frightened.'

Unsatisfactory relationships between teachers and pupils

In some instances, relationships between teachers and pupils had been unsat-isfactory. There were instances of relationships which had been excessively strained, or too relaxed and insufficiently challenging. In all these cases, the result was that the pupils were insufficiently motivated to learn and/or to become involved in the life of the school. In some schools, there had been little recognition of the need to provide pupils with equal access to educa-tional opportunities. Those we interviewed talked of pupils not responding well to the teaching they received. Often pupils had been very restless or passive and had shown little interest or pride in their work or in the school. Pupils had demonstrated little respect for others and for their property. Their persistent poor behaviour often disrupted the learning of others and the smooth operation of the school. In one extreme case, one headteacher of a primary school had 'found anarchy in the school' on taking up her appointment. The staff, who despaired of their poor relationships with a small number of badly behaved pupils, had appeared to be powerless to deal with the situation. In the view of this headteacher, the situation had been largely the result of there being no clear system of rewards, a lack of consis-tency among staff in imposing discipline, and little backing from senior management for attempts by members of staff to confront inappropriate behaviour. As one teacher at the same school recalled:

> When the new headteacher first took over, the school was at its lowest ebb ever. Indiscipline was at a very high level. The children were dread-fully behaved. We couldn't get supply teachers to cover. The teachers here used to go to meetings and be ashamed to admit where they taught.

Low pupil self-esteem and self-confidence

A significant theme was that insufficient attention had been paid to the well-being of individual pupils who suffered from poor self-esteem. Few, if any, serious attempts had been made to promote the development of the pupils' self-confidence. Within their day to day work, teachers rarely trusted pupils to take on responsibilities in class or to become involved in other activities around the school. While extra-curricular activities had been provided in all schools, often only a small minority of pupils had taken part. Few schools had provided pupils with additional support for homework or study. Pupils had not been actively encouraged to become involved in school life in its widest sense, to express their own views, or to value and respect the views of others. Teachers rarely recognised or praised pupils' achievements either individually or publicly in an effort to improve their motivation. Incentives had not been considered appropriate. Some schools had actively opposed reward schemes as they had considered them to be 'over indulgent'. Where pastoral care structures and systems had been in place, they had often been linked insufficiently to pupils' academic progress and development. In general, many teachers had not seen pupil involvement as having a role to play in improving school effectiveness.

Poor attendance

In many schools, there had been a high level of truancy among the pupils, and in some cases a high level of absenteeism among staff. The head-teacher of one school described the attendance of staff shortly after taking up his appointment as 'appalling'. Systems for monitoring and following up pupil absences had often been inadequate. Long-term and persistent short-term absenteeism of pupils had been having a detrimental effect on levels of achievement. The impact of this absenteeism had not fully been appreciated by many parents who condoned their children's absences. The headteacher in one secondary school described a particular case where a pupil had missed the equivalent of eight weeks' schooling each year over a five-year period. This pattern of absence had totalled virtually a whole year of the child's education. The school had had great difficulty in gaining support from the pupil's parents for their efforts to improve attendance. In some schools, there had been a tendency to redefine truancy as condoned absence, because to acknowledge the former would have required an investigation of the reasons for high levels of absenteeism. Poor punctuality had also been a cause for concern in many schools.

Reflecting on the attendance of pupils in the past, one teacher described a situation where the system for following up absences had been inadequate. He recalled that:

There were some pupils whose attendance was absolutely diabolical and who never, ever, seemed to get further than the warning letter. There was no follow up. Pupils got away with it. That was a major frustration for us. You knew that the pupils were thumbing their noses up at us. It was really frustrating. We weren't helped by the fact that taking a day off here and there didn't seem to be a problem for a number of the pupils at this school and for a number of their parents who condone what the pupils are doing. It gets worse until, when they have examination pressures, they tend to opt out. They vote with their feet. They say they can't do it. Really, you're sure that if they had been at school for a bigger percentage of the time, they could certainly have a much better crack at it than they were having.

Lack of a sense of community

Schools in the pre-acceleration phase had often suffered from a poor sense of community. Pupils and teachers had had little pride in, or loyalty to, the school. Contact between the school and the local community had been minimal. Frequently, the notion of community had been viewed in a restricted way. The community was simply the parents and governors. Visitors had not always been welcomed. In general, the local community, including the governing body, had held very low expectations. The various members of the school's community had had little understanding of what the school might achieve or how they could contribute to raising standards. Even when faced with major financial problems, headteachers in some schools had often received only limited support from the governors when putting forward strategies for solving the problems. Some headteachers had, however, been happy with the minimal involvement of governors as it enabled them to exercise greater control over school matters. This strategy of course had disadvantages, particularly in the way it limited the potential for scrutiny of the school's affairs and reduced the pool of expertise available to the management of the school.

In many schools, links with the wider community had been poor. Where links had existed, they had rarely been used as a resource to enrich the curriculum or to widen pupils' horizons. Pastoral links had often been well developed for pupils transferring between schools at nursery, primary and secondary levels. However, insufficient attention had been given to ensuring adequate curricular continuity and progression. At secondary level, links with other educational and training organisations, the careers service and employers had not been well developed. In general, many schools had operated in isolation with only limited opportunities to learn from one another.

Lack of parental involvement

The ethos of schools had often been reflected in the school's day-to-day relationships with parents. Teachers had blamed the low expectations of parents for the unsatisfactory performance of pupils. Parents had often been seen as part of the problem that the school faced. Many members of staff had assumed that parents had little interest in education and even less in becoming actively involved in the education of their children in the classroom or at home. Many teachers had failed to recognise that the opposite might have been true, and that many parents might have had a high regard for education and an interest in their children's school.

Staff in some schools had often underestimated the skills and talents of parents, and in many cases had been happy to perpetuate the clear division that had existed between home and school. Consequently, few schools had made any effort to involve parents actively in their work. Typically, the schools had provided parents with only a minimum of information about school life, the curriculum and their children's progress. Contact between school and home had often been infrequent and usually ineffective. For example, while parents had been expected to support and help their children's learning through homework, few had been provided with the information to enable them to do so. The views of parents had not been considered important, and in many cases they had not been made to feel welcome in school.

While parents may not have been well informed about what makes a good school or how they can help their children, they had often been concerned. They had known that their child's school had major short-comings, or had reservations about the quality of education provided. These concerns had caused some parents to consider alternative provision for their children. The comment of one parent confirmed the position of many parents who had had concerns. She recalled that:

> It used to be that if anyone asked me where my daughter went to school I felt ashamed to say. The discipline in the school was terrible. I considered sending my son to another school when he reached school age. The children here were wild. There was some bullying; it got very nasty at times.

By way of contrast, however, there were examples where parents had not supported a new headteacher in bringing in change to improve pupil achievement. For example, one newly appointed headteacher attempting to establish high expectations among parents found that: 'A small core strongly resisted and resented the new order. They were very, very vocal in their opposition and hostile to what they perceived as my middle class values. There were many face to face exchanges.'

Some interpretation and sense-making

The institutional transformation perspective outlined in Chapter 4 can give some insights into the challenges the schools faced. The fact is that the starting conditions the schools faced did not happen by accident. There were reasons for the condition they were in: some rational but many non-rational, some conscious but many unconscious and hidden. This section of the chapter picks out a selection of the challenges the schools faced and attempts to interpret them and make sense of what was going on. The main themes in this interpretation are the concept of the primary task; social defences against emotion, especially anxiety; roles; group tendencies; systemic thinking; system feedback; boundaries and boundary management.

One of the main themes in the challenges the schools faced at the start of their journeys was failure to address purposefully and to focus sharply on the primary tasks of the institution: teaching and learning. As discussed earlier, both teaching and learning have high levels of emotion, particularly anxiety, associated with them. So, it is almost to be expected that defences will be raised against the emotions associated with those primary tasks. Failure to address the primary task of teaching is very closely linked with withdrawal from the role or the set of behaviours required to achieve a task. So one way of defending against the anxieties of the primary task is to limit and restrict those behaviours. This defence is in effect to withdraw from the role.

Having low expectations of pupil achievement was a standpoint of many of those involved, including some parents. Having low expectations is a way of defending against the primary tasks of teaching and learning. By discounting the primary tasks, effectively before they are started, the emotions associated with the tasks are avoided. The defence is 'I won't attempt the primary task because I know it is not achievable'.

Blaming the pupils' parents is also a defence. It shifts the responsibility for failure in the primary tasks of teaching and learning from the school and the teachers to others. The defence is 'It's not worth attempting to teach the children because their parents are not interested'. Criticising the parents also again helped to discount the primary tasks with the defence: 'Why bother when the parents are not interested?'

The lack of adequate resources for teaching and learning may also be interpreted as discounting the primary task. Here the defence is 'It's not worth attempting to teach the pupils because we do not have adequate resources'. This defence was taken to the extreme in the example of usable and potentially helpful teaching resources being locked away in a cupboard.

Absenteeism on the part of teachers, and truancy by pupils, can also be viewed as a withdrawal from the primary tasks of teaching and learning. The failure to pursue absent pupils and staff is a collusion with the social defence that absenteeism and truancy represent.

The issue of the lack of collegiality and the practice of 'teaching behind closed doors' can be also be interpreted as a defence against the emotion associated with the tasks of teaching and learning. It represents a way of containing and limiting the task-related emotion. This isolation protected the teachers from the emotion that comes with the scrutiny of others as they undertook the task of teaching. It gave a defence against any feelings associated with negative judgements and with being confronted with the potential for change. Teaching behind a closed door allows self-referencing to occur, where teachers judge their own practice by their own standards. This interpretation is also a defence mechanism.

Similar explanations could underpin the lack of interest in, or perceived need for, professional development. Learning to do the primary task differently would mean change (and hence emotion), risk in trying something new (again with an emotional association), and a reminder that the task of teaching and bringing about learning is achievable. This reminder attacks the social defence of low expectations. Any development may also attack the social defences that have been put in place to manage the emotions associated with the primary tasks. For example, beginning to plan collaboratively involves setting aside the defence of teaching behind closed doors.

Another strong theme was the withdrawal from the primary tasks of managing, leading and administering. This withdrawal was evident in the failure to exert managerial authority, to assign responsibility for tasks and to ensure managerial accountability. The management task for the head-teacher, as both leading professional and chief executive, is complex. It is illustrated in the example of the school where the previous headteacher withdrew from the leading professional dimension of his role and retreating into a role devoted to achieving administrative tasks. The example of the lack of non-contact time to manage can be construed as a rational defence against the task of managing. Making sure that managers are not given time to manage can be interpreted as colluding with that 'no time to manage' social defence. A key task of educational management is to ensure that teaching is undertaken appropriately and that learning takes place. Failure to achieve this management task can be interpreted as collusion with those who wish to withdraw from the primary task of teaching.

One feature of the starting conditions of the schools in this study was the lack of positive feedback into all the different systems. As the schools as groups adopted basic assumption tendencies and moved away from task-oriented behaviour, the opportunities for realistic positive feedback also faded. The different sub-systems of the school – the teachers, departments, year groupings, management groups and teams, the governors, the parents and, importantly, the pupils – did not receive appropriate feedback. As a consequence, self-esteem and confidence in being able to achieve the primary tasks of the various groups declined. Very little attention was paid to giving positive feedback to the system, so neither the achievement of the pupils nor the valuable part played by the staff in bringing about that achievement was acknowledged and celebrated. This lack of positive feedback into the systems and sub-systems contributed to undermining any effort to achieve the primary task and the capability to achieve it.

The management of the system boundaries was an important underlying theme in the state of the schools before they began their improvement journey. In many cases, the boundary of the whole school system seemed to be very definitely closed. There was no contact with the school's wider community and the notion of the community was conceived in a very narrow way. It was typically restricted to parents and governors only. The closed and impermeable state of the school system boundary reflected the defended state of many of the institutions. The boundary was not managed in any purposeful or deliberate way. The school's environment was not used as a resource, nor were there many attempts to ensure that the work of the institution conformed to the needs of the environment. In many of the schools, there was even less evidence of the role of the school in leading and managing change in its environment. For example there was little attempt made to educate parents in how to play their part in helping their children to succeed at school.

As discussed earlier, the boundaries of the classrooms remained firmly closed; the classroom door remained shut. Teachers did not discuss their work with each other. There was very little collaboration. There was very little interaction across boundaries with other systems, that is, other teachers, advisory services and professional groups. Teachers worked with their classes in their own classrooms in isolation. At all levels and in all systems, there appeared to be a retreat from the boundary position. This retreat resulted in a withdrawal from the management role, since the boundary is the only place from where the system can effectively be managed and led. The management and leadership of the school played no part in integrating the activities of the school by managing the boundaries of the system or sub-systems. There appeared to be very little systemic thinking.

Concluding comments

This chapter has outlined the kinds of challenge that the schools we studied faced at the start of their improvement journeys. Many of the challenges had overt and explicit reasons. There was a surface rationality to them. Underlying many of those reasons were non-rational explanations. The purpose of analysing those non-rational reasons is to be able to understand them fully and respond to them appropriately. It needs to be reiterated that 'respond appropriately' is, of course, what those in the schools we studied managed to do. All the schools were changing the starting conditions and moving forward on the school improvement journey. The next chapter explores some of the themes in the early stages of the school improvement journeys.

6 Initiating change
Moving into the acceleration stage

Introduction

Beginning the change process was a major task for the schools we studied. Faced with challenges which were often numerous, the schools had to begin to move forward. They had to begin their improvement journey and accelerate the pace of change to bring about improved pupil achievement.

For the schools involved in the project, the movement along the pathway had been initiated by a range of different factors interacting in a different ways. These triggers of change and movement had generally acted in two ways. First, they had initiated some kind of analysis. An example of this kind of trigger is disappointing pupil performance in external examinations in comparison with other similar schools, which had then prompted an exploration of the reasons. Second, the trigger was part of a formal analysis of existing conditions in the school, such as an external inspection or local educational authority review.

This chapter first explores some of the initiators of change and some aspects of the analysis of the conditions in the school in the early stages. It then discusses some of the themes that emerged in our discussions with those who were involved in instituting change and moving the school into a phase where the pace of change began to pick up: an acceleration phase. The chapter then attempts to make sense of the themes and to interpret them from the institutional transformation perspective.

What started the improvement journey?

The schools we studied were chosen because they had all made changes to improve pupil achievement. Understandably, the schools were at different places on their improvement journeys. Also, as we have discussed in Chapter 5, the journeys had had different starting points. The prevailing conditions and cultures had been very diverse at the outset. The triggers for change had also been varied. In some cases, the impetus had been external to the school. These stimuli from outside the school included unfavourable inspection reports or reviews initiated by the local education authority that revealed unsatisfactory practice, or the publication of tables of examination results. In other cases, the impetus for change and improvement had been initiated inside the school itself. Interestingly, in approximately one-sixth of the schools in our sample, the amalgamation of two schools had provided the starting point for renewal and sustained movement along the improvement pathway.

Significantly, in many instances, the initiator of change had been the appointment of a new headteacher and/or other key members of staff, so many of the headteachers in the schools we studied had been in on the beginning of the journey. The appointment of a new headteacher had clearly had a significant effect on many of the schools. Several of those to whom we spoke, including teachers and governors, commented on the initial impact of a new headteacher. One teacher remarked on his experience of a newly appointed headteacher:

> The appointment of a new headteacher is a traumatic experience for a school. I was impressed by the new head's style and energy. It was frenetic, exciting, scary perhaps for some members of staff. Some people can get tired just looking at someone like that! I liked it. Some people did get upset, feathers were ruffled.

The schools, because of their history, their internal conditions and the way these trigger factors combined, had been in varying states of readiness to move forward. Whatever the stimulus, those initiating change had needed to be skilful in using the internal conditions and the stimuli for change to their advantage, to bring about change and to provide a rationale for it.

The importance of initial analysis

Many of the headteachers in the schools we studied had been new to the post of headteacher and many had been new to the school. This 'new head-teacher' factor had generated an interesting paradox for the post-holders. They had had to initiate change rapidly but often had had no grasp of the finer details of their school's circumstances, micro-politics and cultural history. Equally, many of the headteachers – and other members of staff in a number of instances – had seen this lack of awareness as an advantage. It had given an opportunity for the headteachers to examine matters afresh without the baggage of outmoded loyalties, fixed patterns of behaviours and pre-set expectations.

Regardless of the nature and outcomes of the initial analysis, the symbolic acts which represented the imminent climate of change and the 'new' were seen by many respondents as important. The importance of these symbolic acts is extensively supported in the literature on leadership. Among the headteachers we interviewed, many asserted quite clearly the imperative of the new headteachers making an impact as early as possible. By all accounts, these early symbolic acts had to be visible and ideally had to convey a 'values message'. For example, a redecorated staff-room had conveyed a message that the teachers in the school were valued. The first act of one headteacher had been to remove the barbed wire from around the school entrance. This simple action had carried the messages that members of the community were welcome there, and that it wasn't expected that the children would want to escape! Removing the barbed wire from the entrance may also have had added unconscious significance given the importance of boundary management in effective leadership (see Chapter 4).

Despite the value of the early acts symbolising the new order, a consistent and strong theme had been the importance of accurately analysing the prevailing conditions in the school and determining its 'health'. This analysis had helped the new headteacher to adopt the right leadership approach, to set priorities and to plan and implement appropriate strategies for improving pupil achievement.

How was the analysis carried out?

During interviews the headteachers, reflecting on the situation when they took up their posts, described schools that had been at a low base and in much need of improvement (see Chapter 5). In the early stages, the new headteachers had focused their efforts on gaining what they regarded as essential insights into the school's norms, values and beliefs. They had felt they needed to understand the different cultures and subcultures within their schools before they could begin to initiate any major changes. Often they had come to understand their school by talking to the staff, in its entirety, in small groups and individually, by talking to pupils, parents and governors, indeed everyone who had an interest in the school. Unfortunately, few had had the luxury of reflecting for any length of time on what they found. The urgent need for improvement had often forced the pace of change significantly.

Many headteachers at this stage had initiated audits or reviews to determine and provide evidence of the strengths and weaknesses of the school as a whole, and within individual departments and sections. While some schools had used external agencies, such as the local authority advisory service, to carry out the reviews, in many cases the headteacher and/or the deputy headteachers had undertaken them. Successful reviews appeared to have been characterised by:

• ensuring that the process did not further undermine staff confidence
• guaranteeing and maintaining confidentiality
• stressing the developmental purpose of the audit rather than any judgmental or punitive intention.

The use of an audit and reviews in combination with new leadership appeared to have given added authority to any subsequent intended change. It also helped to establish an agreed agenda. By and large, both the headteachers and staff reported positive outcomes of these reviews.

Initiating change: moving into the acceleration stage

A number of changes had been initiated to address the challenges that the schools faced and to begin moving the schools forward. The main themes in the strategies and the strategies themselves are not dealt with in a particular order. Also, it is clear to us that the themes interrelate and overlap. In practice, the ways in which the themes, strategies and practices in the change process were acted out vary according to the context. Also, importantly, the operation of any particular strategy, such as increasing the involvement of parents, will vary and be adapted in different ways along the pathway. Different themes are managed differently at different points along the journey.

Improving the physical learning environment

In many of the schools, there had been an urgent need to focus on teaching and learning as a means of raising levels of achievement. However, for many headteachers, improving the physical environment of their schools had been an early priority. This strategy was particularly important where the physical environment was very unsatisfactory. The changes only needed to be small but they had to be significant. Although the direct impact of these changes on pupil achievement might have been minimal, they often contributed to the development of a 'feel-good factor' and raised staff and pupil morale. In some instances, the changes to the physical environment were more substantial. One headteacher recalled how, within a relatively short time of her arrival, she and her staff had filled forty skips with rubbish from all areas of the school. Displaying pupils' work was also considered to be important, on the basis that new and prominent displays of pupils' work provided a stimulating and attractive environment. Importantly, it also indicated to pupils that others valued their work.

Some schools had been able to provide new facilities by flexibly exploiting their relative autonomy in the management of school finances. A number of the schools had negotiated improved funding from the local education authority. In the schools we studied, improvements to the physical environment included creating a social area for pupils, developing a library/learning resource centre, setting up a drama studio, and constructing new facilities, for example for technology and business studies. Often, changes had not been on such a large scale, but had still had a significant impact. For example, in one school the carpeting of class-rooms had contributed significantly to improving morale. Even minor improvements to the physical environment were often seen as very public and significant 'icons of the new order.' In the words of one headteacher:

> We pushed on with refurbishment against the odds with no money. People need to have real proof that you can do it. We involved the teachers, the governors and parents in painting parts of the school. That really set the ball rolling. Team building and determination. Even the MP came to show that he was supporting us. The kids will tell you that the school is so much better now.

Almost without exception, in the schools we studied, improving the physical environment of the school was a priority.

Changing the school culture

Although improving the physical environment had been a significant priority, most of the newly appointed headteachers knew that their real work was in planning and initiating change in the learning conditions and the learning culture of the school. Intuitively, it seems that the headteachers had recognised the significance of changing the culture. They realised that an organisation's culture can constitute a brake on change for improvement. These head-teachers were aware that for improvement to begin to occur, they needed to change the existing culture and to align it with their vision for the school.

In many of the schools, cultural change and the 'journey' metaphor were used in two senses. In the first sense, for example, there might have been a desire to improve pupil achievement. In this sense, the end-point of the journey would be viewed in terms of *outcomes*. In another sense, the vision was concerned with achieving a new *process,* which one headteacher described as one of moving the school from: 'one which was stagnant to one of continuous improvement.' This perspective would see the end-point of the journey as a change in the process.

Articulating the vision

In moving schools along the improvement pathway, the primary focus had quickly become a sharing of the 'vision' of what the school could achieve in the future, and of developing a 'common mission' to achieve the vision. Many headteachers in the study stressed the importance of articulating the vision and the goals of the school at every available opportunity, constantly and consistently, to staff, to parents and to pupils. Articulating the vision was for them a major activity, as this account by one teacher indicates:

> The new headteacher shared the 'vision' with staff of where the school was at and where it could be in five years. Staff meetings were followed

up by meetings with individual heads of year/heads of department; at each, their current roles and responsibilities were discussed and the contribution each would make to achieving the vision. It was the first time that issues of accountability had been raised. In turn, the heads of year/heads of department discussed these issues at departmental meetings. The headteacher interviewed all the staff along similar lines – including non-teaching staff. These interviews enabled the headteacher and staff to take stock of one another. The vision was then shared with pupils and parents.

A key factor in raising expectations had been convincing all of those involved that improvements could be made, and that each and every member of staff had a contribution to make and would be held accountable. As one headteacher indicated:

> The key dynamic for school improvement is a vision of what you want to achieve and the capacity to sustain it. It is the capacity to show others, to win over others to the notion that school improvement is attainable. We have to show them that we have the skills and the capacity to achieve and then to identify the key systems that can help us to achieve it. The pupils are aware that there will be no hiding place. The staff are aware that it is our key function to improve. . . . At the end of the day, raising achievement and trying to ensure that the children achieve the very best they can, is the absolute priority in this school.

Another headteacher made a similar point:

> Raising standards is not something you can just pull down out of a suitcase and dust down every now and then. Raising standards has to be a theme which permeates all that we do. It is something that is continuously reinforced.

Articulating the vision had clearly been important in initiating change to improve pupil achievement.

Leading resolutely and resiliently

Having strong convictions is a well-established element of effective leadership, particularly in those leaders seeking to effect cultural change. However, the determination and courage shown by some of the headteachers in the study, as they dealt with difficult issues, surprised us. Of course conflict and disagreement are inextricably linked with complex institutional change. In a small number of the schools we studied, by all accounts the resistance to change had been very strong, with some members of staff displaying outright hostility to the proposed changes.

In some schools, the extent of the culture change had been substantial, and the range and depth of the responses to it varied in extent. One head-teacher explained the resistance to a change in approach by some of his staff as follows:

> These people have lived in an environment which was teacher centred rather than child centred. It is very difficult to bring people like that around. Implementing change – 5 per cent of people can be changed overnight; within six months maybe 55 per cent will change to a new way of working; 35 per cent will take an extended period of up to two years. The remaining 5 per cent are 'mentally retired.' You'll never change them. I firmly believe that there are people who will not change. They don't fit in.

In another school, the headteacher described his experience in the early days after he took up his post, and the complex and taxing nature of the task that had faced him:

> When I took over, I suspect that most of the staff were negative; some wanted things to change, but didn't know how to do it. Managing the school situation was totally unbelievable. Sometimes it was a step at a time, an hour at a time. The culture shock to some of the staff has been phenomenal.

Not all the resistance to change had come from members of staff. In some cases, the opposition had come from unexpected quarters such as parents, who resented the headteacher's attempts to raise expectations. There were instances where the resistance had come from the governors who, following their appointment of the new headteacher, had backed away from supporting the changes the headteacher was initiating to improve pupil achievement. For some of the headteachers, these kinds of experience had led to a sense of extreme isolation that only began to ease as the staff were 'won over', or through the appointment of new staff. The personal cost to many of the headteachers had been high. For example, the headteacher in one school indicated that: 'With so little support inside the school, it was very hard to make changes. I was out there on my own. I didn't have a full night's sleep for many months.' Another new headteacher gave the following advice:

> You can never rest. It's very time consuming. It is essential to retain your enthusiasm and sense of humour. But, it's never ending. The secret is to keep your anxieties from everyone else . . . you must get the message across in a very up-beat positive way.

The management of change had, in some cases, called for extreme determination and resolve. It also demanded high levels of resilience on the part of those leading the change.

Dynamic flexible leadership

From the data collected during the study, it was clear that the headteachers who had been successful in managing change were able to deploy a dynamic and flexible style of leadership that enabled them to deal in very different ways with different individuals, at different times and in different situations. This contingent leadership behaviour appeared to be important in the short, medium and long term.

Building 'leaderly relationships' with individual members of staff was clearly important. One new headteacher had had to make an immediate reduction in staffing levels following her appointment, which had made the process of building of relationships difficult. She summarised her approach as one of: 'Building up relationships on an individual level by undertaking a charm offensive on a one to one basis. It took a very long time to be accepted by staff.'

Many of the headteachers espoused the use of a wide range of leadership styles and concluded that there was no particular winning way. Adaptability was important. One headteacher, who took over a school with major problems described the variation in his leadership style over a period of time. He considered that he had been: 'Autocratic in the beginning. There was little consultation with staff. The immediate concern was to gain credibility among the staff, pupils and parents.' He considered that his style had now changed dramatically from his early approach. The same headteacher stressed that he had worked hard to restore staff morale and self-confidence, and the school now prided itself on its effective team approach and good working relationships.

Another headteacher pointed to the use of different leadership approaches as appropriate to the circumstances, and also hinted at the difficulty of choosing and acting out the different approaches: 'It's a narrow line. Sometimes you have to use a "top down" approach and at other times a "bottom up" approach. The balance that works in this school may not work in another.'

The importance of valuing the past in managing radical change was also important, and had been used to good effect by some headteachers. It had been particularly significant in those schools we studied which had been formed by the merger of two schools. The creation of a new school obviously demanded that new basic systems were established. However, the headteachers of merged schools in our sample were careful to retain some of the old to provide a sense of history and continuity:

The amalgamation of two schools is generally an onerous exercise. They both have their separate identities. You need to get a corporate identity to bring the two together. We always wanted it to be a merger not a take-over. The merger gave us opportunities to move forward on a number of counts. Although management were sensitive to staff feelings, it is obvious that there were, and in some cases still are, difficulties.

A member of staff agreed that the difficulties continue: 'There was, and to some extent still is, a split within the staff. Staff from School A have seen their status and role eroded and changed totally. To them the merger was in fact a mugging.'

Initiating the development of a collaborative culture

Many of the headteachers we spoke to had endeavoured to create a more collaborative way of working in order to make progress on the improvement journey. Overcoming unsatisfactory interpersonal relation-ships between members of staff had been important in achieving a more collaborative culture. The common and accepted practice of teachers working in isolation had also had to be addressed. Faced with these chal-lenges, many of the headteachers had devoted considerable time and effort to developing trust and openness among staff. The visibility of the head-teacher and the members of the senior management team had been important in creating this open and collaborative environment. It was important for them to be visible around the school and in the staffroom. On appointment, one headteacher had immediately relocated her office to a more central position so that she had easier access to staff and pupils and they had easier access to her.

A number of diverse strategies had been used to introduce changes in the curriculum, to break down teacher isolation, encourage a collaborative approach and empower staff. Efforts had been made to increase and enhance the professional dialogue in the school and to improve communi-cation at both formal and informal levels. Regular and frequent meetings, including daily briefings, subject team and middle management meetings, and the production of in-house newsletters, all made a significant contri-bution. The professional dialogue and two-way communication were particularly important where there had been strong resistance to change. In some cases, it was necessary for the headteacher to reduce the power and influence of those who were hostile to change, unwilling to develop productive working relationships and/or unable to collaborate.

The need to meet National Curriculum requirements was reported by headteachers as a useful lever in moving their schools forward. The imple-mentation of the National Curriculum affected every member of the teaching staff, and there was no alternative but to adopt it and use it. Although implementing the National Curriculum perhaps represented an imposition on and challenge to the staff, implementation was a valuable and helpful task. The teachers were obliged to implement the National Curriculum. However, they could only introduce it and integrate it into their practice by working collaboratively.

Team activities that encouraged collaborative working were typically substantial practical activities such as the development of new schemes of work or policies. Often, for the first time, teachers from a number of teams worked together on specific whole-school tasks that enabled them to share not only the workload but also ideas and expertise. While the tasks varied in nature, all were real and important activities. Tasks that promoted collaboration successfully were not artificially contrived merely to get the teachers to work together.

Where two schools had amalgamated, the physical task of moving, sorting and arranging the teaching resources often played an important first step in developing a cohesive, collaborative team-based culture. One school had found it helpful to include all staff when forming groups to work on specific issues. By including both teaching and non-teaching staff, from each of the former schools, they were able to 'break down the camps'. This process in turn had helped to develop a whole-school view of the way forward. In this case, from the beginning, all members of staff had been fully involved in formulating the school development plan. This full involvement had not only created a strong sense of ownership among staff, but also ensured that everyone focused on the same agreed targets.

Many headteachers described the importance of identifying a small number of key people and working alongside them to begin implementing improvements 'a small step at a time'. It was important that this 'change group' was identified quickly. Often the improvements focused on things which were relatively easy to change, such as designing a new school uniform. Evidence of success not only demonstrated that change was possible and that the school was changing, it also encouraged staff, pupils and parents to become actively involved in the change process. A successful strategy used by many newly appointed headteachers was to identify positive features of the schools which were used to promote the self-esteem and morale of staff. One headteacher offered the following advice:

> It was very important at the beginning to praise what the school had done in the past, what the staff had achieved; to build their self-esteem. It was important not to go in and denigrate what had gone on before; not to denigrate the school or the catchment area. We (senior management) made sure that staff were fully involved in everything we did. This approach was new to the school. The attempts to involve staff and the heads of faculty/department at an early stage in all new initiatives were deliberately designed to make them less threatening. There were no secrets.

In many cases, the development of a collaborative approach to effecting change to improve pupil achievement had been considered important.

Encouraging the creativity of staff

Encouraging staff to be creative and to generate new ideas was an important theme. In many instances, particularly where staff had been anxious about change and where morale (and therefore confidence) had been low, the headteacher and other key staff had worked alongside teachers in developing new initiatives. In adopting this approach they were, in the words of one headteacher, 'sharing the risks'. Supporting staff and encouraging them to try new methods or initiatives had proved to be very useful in piloting new ideas. In this way, problems could be overcome before extending the new initiatives throughout the school. It had also helped to create a culture of change and a climate where change was accepted. One new headteacher described the benefits of this approach:

> We try to support initiatives. If the staff come along with a good idea we try to run with it if we have the resources. It is important to support initiatives. The last thing I want staff doing is sitting up in the staffroom thinking there is no point going to him. He'll not help. We've gone with some ideas in the past that have later collapsed. That's part of the learning curve! Then we have gone with other things that we have thought might not come to a marvellous end. Things that have really blossomed. You have to be creative and take risks sometimes. It's a learning experience.

The approach of encouraging creativity, risk-taking and not pointing the finger of blame when people made mistakes is encapsulated by the comments of another headteacher:

> It is important not to punish mistakes. Important not to set up a culture where people are reluctant to try things; staff need to be encouraged to be innovative, to take a risk. You have to accept that some of these might not come off. In the same way that they mistakes, I make mistakes myself and I expect support from the staff.

Using data and evidence

It had often been necessary to provide 'hard' evidence of pupils' achievements or lack of them to convince staff – and others occasionally – of the need to raise the level of achievement. A teacher in one school described how:

> The headteacher ensured that staff could see the evidence of the need

for change when he pinned the school performance tables to the staffroom wall. These showed that a neighbouring school had a greater percentage improvement. This jolted many staff into change!

Many members of staff had found it uncomfortable when their low expectations were challenged. This discomfort was most difficult when in some schools it was pointed out that while the pupils' achievements in public examinations might not have declined, their achievements had not been improving as in other schools. This approach of using data to point out the need to change had been new to many staff. The use of data had successfully illustrated the need for improvement. As one secondary school teacher indicated:

> Another change in recent years is that we are all aware of where we are regarding league tables and performance indicators. Until recently, I wasn't aware that we were being compared with anybody other than schools within the same county. . . . Now we are all aware of performance indicators. We are all in a competitive market and with staff this creates a more united effort to improve. It's almost as if we close ranks. It appears that staff are working towards a common goal. We all are. We are trying to improve, year on year.

The use of data to point up the need for change had clearly been important in initiating change.

The use of external sources of influence and support

In managing change during this phase, many headteachers had made increased use of external sources of influence and support. A high level of support from the local education authority staff, including those at senior levels, was seen by many headteachers as important. It had been a very visible and valuable source of influence to support change for improvement. In seeking to implement radical changes, many headteachers had made extensive use of the local education authority advisory and support service. It had proved valuable in meeting the pressing needs of schools as well as providing guidance on strategies for improvement and access to innovations. Many headteachers reported that they had found the help and support of highly committed governors to be invaluable. It was particularly helpful as they struggled to overcome resistance and manage the change process. This support and expertise was especially valued in those instances where governors with experience of industry and commerce were able to offer the headteacher expert advice. This expertise was particularly helpful in cases involving major financial problems or personnel issues.

In general, most governors were themselves on a steep learning curve as they sought to take on new approaches and systems. This issue was particularly significant for new governors, who had to familiarise themselves not only with educational issues and their responsibilities, but also with being a governor of a school undergoing significant change. The governors we spoke to indicated that the training provided by the local education authority, particularly on participation in formal meetings, had been very beneficial.

Improving relationships with pupils

An early priority for the schools involved in the project was to improve relationships between staff and pupils, both in and out of the classroom, and from their responses they had made considerable efforts to do so. Reflecting on the importance of good relationships, one headteacher indicated that:

> You can start from the premise that all pupils are disruptive little devils and you had better stamp on them before they get out of line. Or you can operate from the opposite standpoint: that all pupils are fundamentally co-operative. The approach you take is quite critical. It is the message you give pupils. It is the way we deal with individuals. All of it is based on the quality of relationships. They are a strength of this school. It's an adult type of relationship, based on mutual respect. It is particularly about maturity, tolerance and mutual understanding. It is just there. The pupils rarely take advantage. . . . The vast majority of pupils at this school are very pleasant, co-operative and helpful.

The view of Year 11 pupils in the same school supported this general stance, as these comments from one pupil indicated:

> The teachers here are great. They communicate well with pupils. In other schools they just teach and that's that. Here they're great. Very approachable. When you talk to them about a problem, they put themselves in your position. That's how they help us. . . . It's important to staff that pupils are happy. They know us well and would notice if you changed your personality or the way you work.

Improving pupils' self-esteem and self-confidence

The improvement of the pupils' self-esteem and confidence had been an early priority. In many schools, the management of the pastoral care of pupils had been improved and integrated with day-to-day teaching. In many secondary schools, Personal and Social Education (PSE) had been timetabled and the teaching of PSE involved the whole staff. Senior staff members had been included in the teaching of PSE. They contributed in areas where they had significant strengths and interests.

The organisation of new and more appropriate pastoral care systems reflected the change of emphasis from one of 'care' to one which linked strongly with pupils' academic progress. Ongoing monitoring and assessment had provided pupils and their parents with accurate and up to date information on their progress and well being. New staffing structures to improve the pastoral care system had been put in place in some cases. For example, in one secondary school a house system had been changed to a year system, where year heads were responsible for a whole year group instead of cross-year groups. The intention was that the year heads would continue to have responsibility for a specific year group as the pupils progressed through the school. In this way, the staff not only got to know pupils well, but the pupils' academic progress was more effectively monitored. The members of the teaching staff had been encouraged to promote the pupils' self-esteem and self-confidence and to develop positive attitudes in the pupils through day-to-day teaching and learning.

Celebration of achievements

In the early stages of the school improvement journey, every opportunity had been taken to celebrate publicly significant changes, success and achievement in academic and non-academic areas. Those we spoke to considered that it had been important to convince pupils and staff that they could achieve, and in the words of one respondent to 'make them believe in themselves'. This approach had been seen as a necessary complement to raising expectations. Many schools indicated that they had deliberately set out to have a high public profile. Every opportunity had been used at both primary and secondary level to involve pupils and to make them believe in themselves; that they could and would achieve. The response of one head-teacher summarised the rationale for this approach. He considered that:

> You need to encourage participation and reward it. It is all about engaging children and knowing that these things are very important to children. Praise encourages and motivates pupils and gives them confidence to improve and extend themselves.

Some interpretation and sense-making

Of all the transitions in the improvement journey, arguably 'getting the school moving' is possibly the most challenging. Clearly the triggers that start the journey play an important part, but what did those triggers do? One interpretation is that they all in some sense 'fractured the culture'. For a moment, they altered the rituals, changed the rules and broke the routines that made up the way the institution went about its business. The political climate was disturbed, and the relationships and the power positions that had developed over a period of time momentarily became disordered. At that point, where anxiety is heightened, new alliances and relationships may be formed and therein lies an opportunity for a skilful leader. The trigger creates a brief moment when the social defences that have grown up in the school and become part of the daily goings-on are exposed and possibly opened up. There are two significant dimensions to this process. First, the initiator of change possibly brought a fresh perspective on accepted practice in the school, so that the prevailing culture was exposed to scrutiny. It asked the question 'Are we doing the right thing?' Second, the trigger perhaps brought an expectation of change. It raised the possibility that things would be different.

The pulling and release of the trigger – the firing of the starting pistol – can be a critical moment for the school, and is likely to be associated with very high levels of emotion and anxiety. The responses of individuals and groups in the school and the key stakeholders will depend on the internal conditions in the school and the internal conditions, the mind-sets, of individuals in the school. Those individuals who are hungry for change will be energised; those who are not may be fearful and anxious. Their response to the threat will be to fight it or to flee from it. They may respond to these anxieties with anger, and the behaviour they present may be one of hostility, resentment and bitterness. They may seek to deny that there is a problem and to ignore the issues that are being raised. The emotions aroused in defence against change will be potent because they have three powerful dimensions.

First, there will perhaps be a concern that individuals, groups, the whole institution will be called upon to focus on the primary task (which carries anxiety). In the case of an under-performing school this primary task will be teaching and learning.

Second, there is a concern that they will be asked to dismantle their social defences against these anxieties linked to the primary task. For example, they may be called upon to raise their expectations of the pupils.

Third, the dismantling of the social defences and the re-focusing on the primary task will involve change, and the response to this change will have an emotional dimension. All this emotion must be worked with and contained. The containment of the emotions is the central change management role and of course, the key leadership role.

Already, a central theme to emerge from this study is that the leadership role is a special one. It is special because the primary task of leadership is to enable others to engage purposefully in their own primary tasks. These ideas are developed further and the issue of the leadership of educational change is dealt with in greater depth in Chapter 9.

As in Chapter 5, the following section explores some of the themes in the change process from the institutional transformation point of view. To recap, central concepts in institutional transformation are the concept of the primary task; social defences against emotion, especially anxiety; roles; group tendencies; systemic thinking; system feedback; boundaries and boundary management.

Improving the physical environment was a strong theme in many of the cases we studied. Making improvements directly and indirectly injects positive feedback into the systems and the sub-systems of the school. This feedback boosts the processes of the system. The display of pupils' work – one frequent improvement to the appearance of the school – had sent powerful messages to staff, parents, pupils and visitors that the pupils' work deserves to be seen by others. Such displays also improved the self-esteem and confidence of the pupils, which was another strong theme. Improvements to the buildings also gave positive feedback to the teaching staff. They conveyed a message that the members of staff deserved to work in a pleasant environment. Improvements to the physical environment also communicated messages about leadership authority and leadership effect-iveness, especially when the improvements were secured through additional funding or astute financial management.

The use of external influence and support in other ways had been important in establishing and enhancing leadership authority. In some instances, the improvements had also impacted on the achievement of the primary tasks of teaching and learning. How can a school which keeps sufficient rubbish to fill forty skips be a place where learning can occur effectively?

One other benefit that comes from improving the physical environment is that it sends a message that 'things around here are going to change'. Learning to live with change is a significant part of the change management agenda, and developing that capability to live with change is a significant part of the development of the school.

At an unconscious level of course, improving the fabric of the school and clearing out rubbish perhaps served other purposes. They both image in different ways what may be key unconscious motives and desires. The repair of the fabric of the school may have resonated with a desire to repair internal fragmentation and discomfort by creating a whole and valuable external object of worth and merit. This notion of reparation, first developed by Melanie Klein, may be an explanation for the extreme commitment that many of the successful headteachers had to the task of 'repairing' their schools. This issue is explored further in Chapter 10. The clearing out of the rubbish may have symbolised the removal of the clutter and rubbish of the social defences that had built up to prevent a full engagement with the primary task.

The issue of culture change is an interesting one. Arguably, all the change that took place was culture change. It was fundamentally a 'change in the way we do things round here'. Any change, however, is viewed from the perspective of the existing culture. Strong cultures can filter new ways of looking at the world through the old ways, often generating a disbelief system. This disbelief system is grounded in the ways of thinking and acting that constitute the highly resistant social defences set up to cope with the emotional difficulties associated with the primary task.

Even at this early stage of the journey, the true nature of the change brought about in these schools starts to become clear. The schools were beginning to move from being ineffective and static to being effective and capable of changing to improve. This change is the essence of the journey, and as we have already discussed represents a transformation. The ramifications of this transformation for effective leadership are explored further in Chapter 9. Articulating this vision of what the end-point of this change would be was clearly important, and featured in the accounts of many of the headteachers. Likewise, the common mission, that is, some notion of shared work with a joint purpose, was important. This articulation of the vision perhaps represented an attempt to specify the purpose of the system for which the leader was responsible.

The nature of leadership authority is interesting in this stage. Firstly, leadership authority appeared to be marked by extreme flexibility of action. The leaders needed to have the capacity to adapt, and their leadership was played out in different ways according to different circumstances. Secondly, leadership authority was marked by extreme resolution and determination. The leaders had had to show very high levels of persistence, conviction and tenacity. There is an apparent paradox here. Leadership actions appear to combine flexibility and adaptability with a total unwillingness to be either flexible or adaptable.

The issue points to two important facets of leadership. First, if a purpose of leadership is to bring about change, then leadership actions must adapt and change over time, because of the change to the context which leadership brings about and in which leadership has then to take place. Leadership actions have to adapt over time if they are to remain effective; that is one of the reasons why it is so difficult to 'capture the essence' of effective leadership.

Second, leadership adaptability in the form of extreme contingency in leadership action is a significant feature of the improvement journey. Where there was willingness on the part of teachers and managers to change and engage in the primary tasks of teaching and managing, there was fulsome praise and support from the leader, typically the head. Where there was opposition, the resistance was resolutely confronted. Vince and Martin's (1993) model of the responses to the anxiety associated with learning and change in groups gives some insights into this practice. Their model, which is illustrated in Figure 6.1, has two alternative cycles. In the first, the amplifying loop, the group or individual lives with the uncertainty and risk associated with change/learning and, through a process of struggle, gains insight and authority. In the other loop the balancing loop, the pathway is characterised by a fight-or-flight defence (a classic biological response to anxiety), which can encompass denial, avoidance, defensiveness and resistance, and leads to a state of willing ignorance. Interestingly, both pathways lead back to anxiety, but anxiety that has different bases and origins. In terms of the leadership of educational

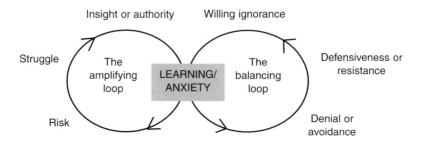

Figure 6.1 Responses to anxiety associated with learning and change

Source: after Vince and Martin 1993

change, the leader contains the anxiety of the other (a teacher or manager) in their work in the amplifying loop. In this way they enable and bring about learning and development. In other contexts, the leader steadfastly refuses to give way or collude with those wishing to engage in the balancing loop process, and as a consequence faces the accompanying individual and institutional projections, such as anger or withdrawal. By supporting others in their attempts to change and by refusing to collude with resistance to change, the leader manages change 'educationally'.

Guiding others – individuals, groups, the whole institution – around the amplifying loop is a key leadership act. The stages and processes associated with the change process, the risks that accompany change, the uncertainties associated with change, and the struggle as the other seeks to come to terms with the meaning of change, all carry high levels of anxiety. As we discuss in Chapter 9, a key leadership role is the containment of this anxiety for others, in order to prevent them from setting up new social defences and/or calling up familiar defences which will prevent change taking place. If successful, though, the changes release energy which had previously been trapped and creativity which had formerly lain dormant.

The development of the collaborative culture is interesting from an institutional transformation perspective. The notion of collaboration as a way of describing the collective actions of the members of the school community featured strongly in our discussions with all those involved in the changes that had taken place in the schools, and it featured at all stages of the journey. In this early stage, a key purpose had been to begin the development of a collaborative culture. A number of issues are important in a consideration of the idea of collaboration.

1   Collaboration breaks down teacher isolation and separation, which

may be a social defence against the anxiety associated with the primary task of teaching.

2   Collaboration may be a new kind of social defence. It shares the anxiety associated with the primary task: 'Better that we face the enemy together than face it on our own'. There is a mutual containment of anxiety. There is a case, though, for arguing that this social defence, if that is what it is, is a more productive one than separation and teachers working in isolation.

3   Collaboration brings a greater depth of expertise to bear on the primary tasks of teaching and learning. It extends and deepens the 'talent pool'.

4   Collaboration reduces the anxiety associated with managing and being managed. Arguably, all forms of democratic and participative approaches to managing are a way of short-circuiting management power. For the manager, the task of management is almost certain to carry anxiety. The experience of being managed also has emotion associated with it for a variety of reasons. Importantly, 'being managed' may require the person being managed to undertake the primary task effectively, a requirement that may call up high levels of anxiety. Those being managed may fear a loss of control.

5   Collaboration is also a form of integration. It is a way of describing the integration of the different sub-systems in the whole institutional system. This integration is an important leadership act and is a theme in the school improvement journey. Integration is central to change management in complex organisations, since successful change cannot take place unilaterally in such organisations. One sub-system's change has to be accommodated by change in another. Such is the nature of organisational learning.

6   Collaboration can also be a 'meaning-making' process which helps those involved to make sense of events, relationships and problems through professional conversations – the new *professional* discourse that became a feature of the schools we studied – and through shared work.

7   Finally, it could be argued that there was, in many of the schools, collaboration of a kind even at the starting point of the journey. It is simply that the collaboration was not productive in an educational sense. It was a 'collusion in mediocrity', a form of collaboration which all the schools we worked with were succeeding in changing. They were achieving a productive collaboration.

The use of data during this stage demands a particular mention. During this stage, data was not used proactively but was used almost on an incidental basis as corroborating evidence of the necessity of change which was possibly driven by other analyses. It was not used to support and monitor change as it tended to be in the later stages of the improvement journey.

Nor was data used to identify change in aspects of the institution's practice, as it perhaps was in the later stages of the journey. Systematic and sustained data collection did not appear to be a significant characteristic of the early stages of the journey.

The management of the boundary of the school was a feature of the early stage of the journey, and figured significantly at all the subsequent stages. In the pre-acceleration stage, the boundary was not managed proactively or effectively. Typically, it remained closed by default, possibly as a defence against change. As the schools attempted to begin their improvement journey, boundary management became significant. Early efforts at boundary management and establishing contacts with the environment focused on gaining support from external agencies to add weight to the requirement for change and to help convey the urgent need for change. The public celebration of evidence of improvement, and enhancing the 'look' of the school, contributed to managing the interface between the institution and its environment.

7 Living with change
The acceleration stage

Introduction

Once the changes set in motion begin to take effect, the school begins to move, and the journey has started. From our discussions with those involved, the school feels different. The context for change is itself changing and the change processes must adapt accordingly. We have termed this period the acceleration stage largely because the pace of change at this time seems to quicken. This quickening of the pace may have been illusory, a reflection of the number of initiatives set in motion, the scope and scale of the changes being implemented and the changed climate in the school, conditions palpably different from those at the start of the journey.

This chapter sets out some of the themes that were features of the schools during this acceleration phase. As in the two previous chapters, there is also a section that attempts to interpret and make sense of some of the events and characteristics of the schools as they continue their journey.

The acceleration phase

From our discussions with senior staff, teachers, parents, governors and pupils, life in the schools during this acceleration phase was characterised by a number of themes.

Leading in a climate of change

In this phase, the leadership style appeared to change. It is as though the schools having started their journeys, did not require quite the same kind of 'push' they needed at the start of the pre-acceleration phase. In many of the schools, 'being new' in some sense influenced early leadership strategies. In this phase, these strategies were influenced by there being a climate of change, by the requirement to maintain momentum and apparently to expand activity on all fronts. With resistance to change largely overcome or at least reduced in scale, the balance tipped in favour of those initiating and managing the change process.

Providing greater opportunities for leadership

During this stage, in many of the schools there was a deliberate attempt to create opportunities for leadership in others, often through new management structures and/or new appointments. The role of middle managers – heads of department in secondary schools and curriculum co-ordinators in primaries – became increasingly important. They were often viewed as key people in the change process. In many instances, the 'location' of leadership moved from the 'top' down to the heads of department/curriculum co-ordinators. A number of authors, including Michael Fullan, subscribe to the view that leadership should be shared across the school. In secondary schools, the heads of department or faculty appeared to have a more influential role with the teachers in their departments, perhaps working more closely with them than in the past. In primary schools, the empowerment of curriculum co-ordinators enabled them to play a significant role in school development. In discussing the leadership role of middle managers in his school, one secondary school headteacher said:

> One of the secrets of school improvement is not just having the vision but having the body of people to communicate it to others. I emphasise to heads of year, heads of department, the fundamental role that they undertake. That they are leaders in their own areas and that they have to lead those areas. Their job descriptions highlight their accountability. In departmental reviews held each year, I concentrate on their leadership role. I talk to them about their staff, their management structures, their development plan and the analysis of their department's results. It's all about giving staff due regard and giving the job that they are doing due emphasis and respect. I try to unleash their opportunities. . . . A better set of heads of department, you couldn't hope to meet anywhere. My senior managers are brilliant. We have an army of people out there who have what we need to enable us to go forward.

Developing collaboration, team work and whole school approaches

In this phase, the increased staff commitment, morale, esteem and motivation helped to engender more of a whole-school approach with a stronger emphasis on communication and team work. In many cases, the energy and enthusiasm of newly appointed staff was a significant catalyst for change. The headteacher and others in leadership roles seemed ready to adopt much more collaborative ways of working.

Improvement initiatives, which had been predominantly top down, increasingly became a combination of top down and bottom up, although the balance in this combination varied between different schools and within individual schools. Planning the development of the school was no longer the task of senior management but involved departments and individual members of staff in planning for change and the setting of targets for improvement. Some schools, describing their first attempts at target setting, indicated that initially they had started off with a wide range of targets and strategies. The head-teachers often regarded the strategies for achieving the targets and the involvement of staff as more important at this stage than the targets them-selves. It was the process that was important. In the words of the head of a school which had undergone considerable change: 'Staff involvement in whole-school planning and a new climate of accountability have made a major contribution to improvement across a wide range of areas.'

In the special schools in the project the development of a team approach was of particular importance, as the large numbers of support staff were viewed as essential members of the 'teaching teams'. The early development of the collaborative approach was also considered essential in schools where the trigger for the school improvement journey had been the merger of two schools. In such schools, the scale of the change for some members of staff was considerable, as their roles and responsibilities in the new merged school evolved. The extent of the change often resulted in the teachers having a sense of anxiety and vulnerability. Senior staff in one amalgamated school reported how they deliberately created working teams composed of staff from both of the former schools:

> We had to ensure that it was a merger, not a take-over. We made sure that there wasn't a group made up solely of teachers or non-teaching staff from one school only. We divided staff so that there were groups of teachers, administration staff, caretakers as well as members of the governing body. This strategy has not only assisted in breaking down 'camps' but ensured that we have a corporate view of the way forward and common practices across the school.

Encouraging professional dialogue and teacher empowerment

In many schools, the discussion of professional matters became more evident in this stage. There was an explicit dialogue among members of staff about teaching and learning, and the ways that teaching and learning could be improved. Many headteachers talked about a rising sense of empow-erment as the teaching staff became more involved in the work of the whole school and able to influence policy and practice. Many respondents referred to this growth in confidence and empowerment within their schools. This change had a significant impact on the culture of the school. The head-teacher of one school which had previously been, in his own words, 'on the verge of failing' indicated that now:

> There is a change of culture within the school – the way we do things here. It has taken a series of small steps to change the school from one

which was stagnant to the one which exists today. Now, it is a progressing and changing school which has moved forward significantly.

This growth of teacher empowerment, a feature of many of the schools, was explained further by another headteacher:

> As a group of professionals . . . so many staff learned a tremendous amount – in really coming on and developing. In the past, they had been flattened, morale-wise by the wrong people speaking up, having power and running the show. Now staff have been empowered.

Sharpening the focus on teaching and learning

As schools progressed on their journey of improvement, the core functions of the school, teaching and learning, were increasingly seen as a major focus for development. In some instances, post-inspection action plans assisted schools in focusing their attention on improving the quality of teaching and learning. Deficiencies in provision were often overcome through restructuring the curriculum to ensure that all pupils were offered equal access to a curriculum that met their individual needs. For example, in one of the special schools in the study, innovative approaches resulted in a radical reorganisation to provide access to the National Curriculum and, where appropriate, to accreditation.

In many instances, the implementation of strategies for improving teaching and learning became the responsibility of all members of staff, particularly those at middle management level. There were examples of teaching teams, especially those that were working well, acting as significant agents of change. Reports of these meetings indicated some very clear benefits. For example, regular team meetings, often attended by a nominated member of the school's senior management team, facilitated the development of a team approach that ensured coherence and consistency. Collaborative planning of schemes of work and individual lessons ensured continuity and helped to facilitate progression. All of the members of staff increasingly had an understanding of what the pupils were expected to achieve. Discussion focused on issues such as meeting the needs of individual pupils, classroom management skills, evaluating teaching and learning strategies, defining a 'good' lesson or determining what makes a 'good' teacher. Where previously staff development activities had focused on whole school issues and on the general professional development of the staff, increasingly they focused on the classroom matters.

The team approach also appeared to contribute significantly to the development of commonly agreed policies and guidelines in a number of areas. For example, in a secondary school, the teachers in one department agreed to record a wide range of information to show the progress of individual pupils over their school career. The use of assessment data to predict the pupils' level of achievement and/or potential low achievement was now well established. Work throughout the year generated its own specific success criteria, which the teachers converted to 'user friendly' language for pupils to ensure that the pupils understood what was expected of them. In the same school, the departments developed an agreed marking policy and a whole department policy on giving feedback. This departmental policy on giving feedback included ensuring that marking always begins with praise and making sure that pupils are provided with feedback which indicates how they can improve their work. In this department the early monitoring helped to ensure that intervention was provided for pupils who required support. The school considered that these strategies appear to have been successful, as the achievements of pupils in external examinations had improved significantly in recent years with no discernible change in the capabilities of the students embarking on examination courses. This particular school also found that the involvement of the senior management team in working with departments to use a range of data in a formative way also made an important contribution to departmental effectiveness.

Evaluating performance

In this acceleration phase, many of the schools began taking their first steps to monitor and evaluate aspects of practice. The processes of finding out what is going on in a school at all levels and then assessing its value are widely accepted as key elements in securing improvement. They are key processes in ensuring that the institution is operating properly: 'doing things right', and working well strategically: 'doing the right things'. Previously, in many of the schools, monitoring and evaluation of the implementation of school policies and practice had been very informal if they existed at all, and had generally been undertaken by senior staff or external advisers only. As the school began to move on its improvement journey, not only did monitoring and evaluation become more appropriate and more of a priority, but middle managers became increasingly involved in the processes. As one headteacher emphasised: 'The casual passing through classrooms by the headteacher only takes you so far. It doesn't provide a basis for solid professional dialogue about quality.'

Some of the schools provided training to enable the heads of department and curriculum co-ordinators to become involved in monitoring, typically through lesson observation. Of those we interviewed, some were very comfortable in this role and reported enthusiastically on the benefits of classroom observation, while others were less comfortable and enthusiastic. Many admitted that before their involvement in lesson observation they did not really know what was going on in classrooms. Some also had a strong belief that all staff should have the opportunity to observe the lessons of colleagues and to learn from their practice. Providing feedback was not always easy. There appeared to be problems with giving immediate individual feedback. None the less, it was recognised that giving positive formative comment was important, as was sharing the outcomes of lesson observation, perhaps anonymously with members of staff.

Commitment to the continuing professional development of staff

Not surprisingly, continuing professional development played an important part in helping schools to make progress on their school improvement journeys. In this early acceleration stage, staff development appeared to have a particular role.

First, there was a change in the way that staff development was managed. Typically, specific funds and time were allocated for the purpose. The policy and practice for staff development became more structured and focused. For example, school development plans were used increasingly to prioritise the identification of the specific training and professional development needs of staff.

Second, there was a change in the way in which staff development was viewed. Respondents referred to many instances where members of staff saw development as an opportunity for professional change and a way of 'unlocking their potential'. The notion of 'going on a course' to escape from the rigours of school life was no longer deemed to be professionally valid.

Third, there was a difference in the nature of staff development and in the participation of staff in development activities. In some instances, attendance at external training courses was restricted by the head-teachers, who would carefully screen information relating to in-service training and development courses. Priority was often given to releasing members of staff from their classes and using the services of external advisors/consultants to work with those members of staff in their own schools. Those we spoke to recalled that the staff generally welcomed this approach. It provided them with greater access to specialist expertise, facilitated their working with other close colleagues, and ensured that the content of any development was directly relevant to their own professional concerns. Professional development activities also took place within the school during regular timetabled professional training days. This approach helped to ensure that existing staff expertise was utilised to the full, and may have had additional unconscious benefits that are discussed later in the chapter. This readiness to draw upon professional expertise became more significant as the staff became more confident. In many schools, the approach was to challenge the teachers to consider their own practice and how it could be improved. This approach was successful when it was used in conjunction with a supportive and valuing professional dialogue. In this phase, these discussions and exchanges appeared to focus increasingly on important educational issues. In many instances, the sharing of good practice was often easier than it had been previously, as collaboration and teamwork had fostered a new atmosphere of trust and openness. Professional development now focused on supporting the teaching staff as they worked on concerns within their own professional practice. As a result, the knowledge and skills they acquired through professional development activities were put to use directly and had an immediate impact.

Professional development activities in this stage were increasingly creative. In one school where scope for promotion within the school was restricted, development opportunities included staff at middle management levels 'shadowing' senior staff to gain skills and experience of new roles and responsibilities. In another school, middle managers joined the senior management team on rotation for a term. This successful initiative was not only enjoyed by the staff concerned, but was also effective and valuable development for middle managers in whole-school issues. It also contributed to the development of new skills and capabilities. Members of staff were encouraged actively to consider their individual career development and the skills they needed to acquire if they were to progress. During the acceleration phase, many headteachers were ready to support in-school improvement initiatives launched by staff. Examples included members of staff working towards higher degree qualifications, for which they were undertaking action research that focused on an issue of significance to the whole school.

Using the Investors in People award

The Investors in People award (IiP) provides a framework for integrating human resources strategy with organisational strategy. In a significant number of schools, it was a particularly useful instrument in managing change. IiP appeared to be particularly helpful in the newly amalgamated schools we studied. It made a beneficial contribution to the development of the school's image as an institution and assisted in the identification of the training needs of all staff, including administrative and support staff. The use of IiP ensured that the training needs of *all* the staff were addressed and that all staff members were fully aware of the goals of the school and the part that they played in realising them. Sponsorship from the local Training and Enterprise Council was a useful contribution to the training costs of non-teaching staff.

Listening to the pupils

The importance of pupil involvement as one of the enabling conditions for school improvement is well established in the literature. In many schools, at the start of the school improvement journey, the views of pupils were sought, if only on a small scale. For example, the children in one primary school were asked what improvements they would like in their school. Understandably, the pupils were very pleased when many of their suggestions were implemented. In the secondary schools in the project, pupils' views were often solicited through informal discussions. To a lesser extent during this stage, pupil views were sought through bodies such as School Councils or Youth Forums. These discussions provided the pupils with opportunities to influence school policies and procedures. The pupils' self-confidence and self-esteem were developed as they represented their peers and the school in a wide range of activities. The Chair of one School Council, a Year 11 pupil, outlined its benefits:

> If any other school were to consider forming a School Council, we would strongly recommend it. It is important that pupils do not think that School Council is somewhere you go with a wish list and expect everything to happen at once. The Council does give you a platform where your views can be heard but it is also important that you listen to the views and opinions of others. The School Council has given us an insight into how the school is run and why various decisions are taken.

According to those we spoke to, these representative forums were most successful where staff believed that the pupils should have a say in the school, respected their views and, were prepared where necessary, to change their own ideas in favour of those suggested by pupils. A head-teacher who felt strongly that pupils should be involved in school improvement issues indicated that:

> Having a School Council is so important because the pupils have got to learn that it's not the teachers' school. It's their school. If we are really going to improve, then everybody has to be involved and the pupils' views respected and listened to.

Through all these mechanisms, the pupils gained important insights into how the school operated and an understanding of the rationale for decisions. There were other benefits too, in terms of the development of the pupils' self-esteem, self-confidence and self-empowerment.

Involving pupils in their learning

In many of the schools, a feature of the early stages of the improvement journey was the active encouragement of pupils to participate fully in their learning activities and to develop as effective learners. The strategies used to involve pupils in their learning varied widely. None the less, an outcome of all of them was that the pupils demonstrated increasingly positive attitudes to their teachers and to their work.

In infant and primary schools, the pupils were often involved in recording evidence of their own achievements in record of achievement portfolios. The introduction of personal organisers or action planners in secondary schools helped the pupils to plan and manage their own learning. These organisers and planners were also a useful mechanism for keeping parents in touch with their child's work and progress. Some of the teachers we spoke to used action planners to assist staff, pupils and parents in identifying a pupil's strengths and areas for improvement. The planners provided an opportunity for giving feedback to the pupils. Teachers shared the criteria for success with pupils. When providing feedback on their performance, the teachers would take care to write positive comments in the planners in an attempt to motivate and encourage pupils. Pupils who were under-achieving were challenged and set their own specific targets for improvement in their work and/or behaviour. While the action planners were regularly checked by form tutors and senior staff, those belonging to pupils who were under-achieving were often monitored by teachers in every lesson. A senior teacher explained:

> We don't just encourage the boys who are under-achieving. We present them with the stark facts that unless they shake themselves up they will not be successful. We support them as they try to improve. They know exactly what is required of them if high achievement is to be realised.

Most schools undertook close and regular monitoring of pupils' progress to ensure that the pupils were meeting targets and to arrange for additional support for those who were under-achieving. In some schools, computer-based systems were implemented to record and analyse the data. In some secondary schools, monitoring assisted staff in predicting potential GCSE grades. Often, pupils who were identified as under-achieving, particularly those at the GCSE C/D borderline, were interviewed and set targets for improvement. In many schools, senior staff carried out individual interviews with pupils in Years 10 and 11. Increasingly, other members of staff were involved in an effort to extend the practice lower down the school. Parents were contacted to enlist their support. Pupils were encouraged to improve through mentoring relationships, discussion about their progress, and guidance about how to improve. As one secondary school headteacher indicated:

> Mentoring takes time and given the number of pupils, is quite a commitment. Where resources are limited, you have to use the resources where you feel they will have most return. In Year 11, the proximity of GCSE examinations does tend to focus pupils' minds. I can see all sorts of arguments against this but I think it is important to focus on a particular ability range – pupils on the C/D borderline. You could ask why we aren't focusing on the pupils predicted to get grades F and G ? I agree, but you have to prioritise. If someone goes from a grade D to a C, it opens their whole career out. The whole of their lives could be changed. It opens doors.

In many schools, pupils also benefited from the additional support provided by student tutors from their local university, the University of Glamorgan. In a number of instances, especially in schools where there was little or no tradition of pupils progressing to higher education, this student tutoring often provided the pupils with useful role models.

Study support

In order to make an early impact on pupil achievement, many schools engaged in a number of initiatives with this specific focus. Many schools provided pupils with facilities for study outside normal school hours, since they recognised that not all pupils have access to study/computer facilities or to appropriate support at home. Although in some schools many pupils were dependent on school transport, this problem had been solved through negotiation with bus companies and with parents. As a result of the often-innovative solutions, it became possible for increasing numbers of pupils to attend after-school activities every afternoon.

Again, in an effort to make early inroads into the problem of raising pupil achievement, teachers were encouraged to hold lunchtime revision classes. There were also examples of teachers running extensive programmes of after-school subject-based activities, homework clubs, study weekends, Easter holiday courses and master classes. Local businesses and the Training and Enterprise Councils sponsored many of these initiatives. Some schools encouraged the development of computerised revision packages to assist pupils in supported self-study.

Improving attendance

In this stage, strategies for improving attendance were given a high priority. Detailed policies were developed in those schools where poor attendance was a particular problem. These policies outlined specific procedures for monitoring attendance and identifying at an early stage those pupils for whom attendance was becoming a particular problem. Where this development was successful, agreed procedures were communicated to pupils and parents and applied rigorously by all staff. Full attendance became the expectation and in some instances, parents who wished to take their children away from the school on holiday during term time did so without the agreement of the school. Many schools, seeking to improve attendance levels, involved pupils in monitoring their own attendance, often at half-termly intervals. Comparisons were made between the level of attendance of individuals, their form class and other forms throughout the school. In some schools, 'attendance competition' was actively encouraged, and those pupils who attained 100% attendance over relatively short periods received rewards such as vouchers for the tuck shop or small gifts. Their high level of attendance was also acknowledged through the award of certificates and congratulatory letters sent to parents. These and similar strategies have proved to be successful in a number of schools.

Some schools used computerised systems to monitor attendance and punctuality. Using such systems, teachers would send information by means of electronic pads directly to the School Office, where the data could be accessed by other staff, such as the school's Education Welfare Officer. Unauthorised absences were rapidly followed up. Where there were particular problems, such as those pupils who had been absent for a long period, planned re-entry strategies were used to support the pupils' return. Good attendance in many secondary schools was also promoted through 'Compact' schemes with the local university, which were sponsored by the Education Business Partnership. Through these schemes, pupils were guaranteed a place at the university if they met certain agreed criteria. Similar schemes were used in a smaller number of primary schools to reduce absenteeism and to motivate pupils. Some schools also successfully negotiated 'contracts' with parents that indicated the expectations of both parents and schools.

Involvement in the school community

A feature of the schools as they began their improvement journey was the use of particular initiatives to facilitate wider participation in the life of the school. Where attempts were made to empower pupils and to involve them in the school community, the pupils rapidly showed a stronger sense of belonging and responded well to opportunities provided to exercise responsibility. For example, in a number of secondary schools, senior pupils assisted with the 'Toe by Toe' or 'Buddy' reading scheme where, for twenty minutes on a daily basis, they supported younger pupils by listening to their reading. Those using these schemes reported two specific benefits. First, it made a significant contribution to improving the reading ages of younger pupils. Second, it improved relationships between pupils in the senior and lower schools. The sixth-formers also benefited as they developed a sense of responsibility and practised their interpersonal skills. Year 12 pupils in a Welsh-medium secondary school assisted staff in the local infants' school with activities designed to encourage the development of the children's oral and writing skills. This joint initiative benefited both groups of pupils. The Year 12 pupils who participated in the tutoring programme could gain accreditation for their experiences through the 'Youth Award Scheme Platinum/Universities Award'. The infant school teachers were very enthusiastic about the scheme. One teacher reported that the children: 'thoroughly enjoy these sessions and their fluency and willingness to speak Welsh have increased tremendously.'

In many schools, the range of extra-curricular activities offered was broadened in this phase. These new activities provided pupils with opportunities to develop new interests and skills, and also built the pupils' self-confidence. These activities were often well supported by both pupils and staff, including senior staff. Often, transport arrangements were changed to ensure that those who required school transport were not excluded. One headteacher explained why in his view it was so important to offer pupils a wide range of extra-curricular activities and to facilitate the pupils' attendance:

> At the end of the day, school is here for the pupils to come and learn and for pupils to develop and grow. We've tried to make it a place of learning, a place of enjoyment. There are a lot of extra curricular activities offered here. We continuously focus on the pupils fulfilling their full potential.

Involving families and governors

The evidence from our data suggests that, as schools began to move along their improvement journey, there was a significant growth in their confidence and enthusiasm for developing effective partnerships between the school, the parents of the pupils and the community in which the school was located. Instead of keeping parents at a distance as in the past, schools now put a lot of effort into removing barriers to involving parents in the work of the school. Parents were no longer considered to be part of the problem, but part of the solution. The focus was on developing formal and informal contacts with parents and others, making the school more accessible and encouraging the teachers to be more approachable. It was recognised that parents had useful skills that would be of value to the school. It was also recognised that the development of relationships with parents and the wider community had the potential to improve standards of achievement and the quality of teaching and learning. Given the nature of the communities served by many of the schools involved in the project, in practice the term 'parents' frequently included not only mothers and fathers but also grandparents and other members of the pupils' extended families.

The strategies used to involve parents were varied and were tailored to meet local needs, expectations and culture. It was clear that, as with so many of the initiatives to improve parental involvement, what works in one school may not work in another. In some infant schools, parents were encouraged to take part in pre-nursery sessions that were held for their children. Some schools adopted an explicit open door policy where parents were welcomed into the school and given easy access to the headteacher and staff. Informal or semi-formal meetings were used to share the school's vision and to raise expectations. Information about the curriculum was shared with parents of both primary and secondary pupils in a number of ways. These included the provision of information booklets and attendance at short training programmes. Typically, these covered the programme of work being followed or specific topics in each curriculum area. For many parents, the new experience of sharing such information was a positive one. Those we spoke to confirmed that it was the first time they felt valued by schools and teachers.

The experience was particularly significant to them when the teaching staff indicated the crucial role that parents can play in helping in their child's education. It also helped to persuade parents that together the parents and the school can make a difference to the child's educational achievements. As one parent indicated:

> I was encouraged by the staff to help him at home. I always thought that reading to my child was not helping him as he had to learn to do it himself. The headteacher told me that he is not too old and that I could help him a lot.

On occasions, schools shared their own resources such as materials and textbooks with parents to enable them to help their children at home. Sharing curriculum information and resources with parents was of particular importance in Welsh-medium schools, where many of the children came from homes where English was the first language. One headteacher described how the teachers involved non-Welsh speaking parents in helping their children.

> Parents often ask us how they can help their children. Some parents worry that they can't read or speak the Welsh language. We encourage the children to take home books and tape recordings of the books which staff have made. We explain to parents how we develop reading skills and try to get them as involved as we can. Some parents are now learning Welsh themselves and they say that they have learnt a lot from the very simple books that their children take home.

The inclusion of parents in school functions such as parents' assemblies, concerts, school outings and fund-raising activities was also encouraged. Where space permitted, some schools provided a parents' room where parents could meet and socialise during the day.

Purposeful management by governors played a key role in supporting the school as it moved forward. A key change in many schools was that the governors became more actively involved through their membership of sub-committees. This shift brought them closer to the operation of the schools and to the detail of the strategy for change. In many schools, members of the governing body were encouraged to visit the school during the day. Members of staff were, however, often reluctant to agree to governors observing their classes in operation. Individual governors usually focused their interests on specific areas of responsibility, and may have had links with particular departments/curricular areas. This special interest was particularly useful where heads of department/curriculum co-ordinators were required to report directly to the governors on a regular basis about their progress in meeting targets. This strategy not only helped to raise the profile of these areas, but also provided the governors with an insight into the complexity of what the school was trying to achieve. It also contributed to the development of a climate of accountability. Governors became increasingly knowledgeable about the life and work of the school, which assisted them in setting challenging but achievable targets for improvement. As the headteacher of a primary school indicated: 'The more we open our doors to governors and parents, the happier I feel. We are working hard to make them feel a part of the school community.'

Linking with the wider network

In seeking to become less isolated, cluster arrangements involving secondary schools and their feeder primary schools were a useful mechanism for bringing local schools together. Where they were most effective, there was real partnership as infant, junior, primary and secondary schools shared and exchanged information and supported one another. Increasingly, such partnerships focused on developing effective curricular, as well as pastoral, transition arrangements for pupils at the relevant key stages. Discussion of teaching and learning strategies and the transfer of accurate baseline data on pupils' prior attainments and attitudes were of particular importance. Shared projects, such as initiatives on literacy, European links and information and communication technologies facilitated the growth of effective collaboration among members of staff at various levels throughout the schools involved. The transition arrangements for secondary school pupils included the transition to work, to further and higher education and to other training organisations. For example, the transition of sixth formers to higher education was promoted through the Higher Education Compact programme in partnership with the University of Glamorgan.

Links with industry and the business community became increasingly important as schools recognised that they and other partners in the local community and further afield had much to learn from one another. For example, one primary school, involved for the first time in enterprise activities, worked not only with parents but with industrialists, finance organisations and other agencies such as the Education Business Partnership, Trading Standards Department and the Patent Office as they set up and implemented their very successful project.

Some interpretation and sense-making

Many of the themes that were evident in the stories we heard in this acceleration stage were continuations and extension of the themes that were evident as the school began their journeys of improvement. For example, collaborative approaches were pursued, and as a consequence collaboration seemed to be more widespread and, in a sense, more sophisticated. It was used in a wider range of ways and in more 'locations' in the school.

Leadership authority became increasingly dispersed throughout the school, which appeared to facilitate change for improvement. This shift in the locale of leadership served a number of purposes.

1   It allowed the headteacher, the *ex officio* institutional leader, to move to the boundary of the whole school system from where s/he could manage the system effectively. From this position, the institutional leader could communicate more effectively with those in the school's environment who had an interest or stake in the work of the school. Communicating with, and ultimately leading, those external stakeholders are key leadership tasks. We discuss this issue further in Chapter 9.

2   The shift in leadership meant that the various sub-systems, for example, the faculties, year groups and departments in a secondary school, could be better managed and led. The person best placed to manage a department in a secondary school is the head of department. The teacher in the best position to manage a curriculum area in a primary school is the curriculum co-ordinator. The growth of leadership and management authority throughout the school helps to ensure closer (and therefore better) management.

3   The whole-school leadership can begin to fulfil the key leadership role of integrating the activities of the sub-systems of the institution. The key leadership task is enabling others to take up and enact their role. This can only be achieved by ensuring that there is clarity as to what that role is in relation to the roles of all the other sub-systems. It is the leader's task to integrate these sub-systems by clarifying their roles, and understanding and communicating the ways in which the different roles interrelate.

The ways in which the schools related to and linked with the different individuals and agencies in their environment appeared to change in a number of ways during this acceleration stage. These are the main ones.

1   The schools appeared to communicate and work with a wider range of stakeholders in their environments. The schools linked with other schools, higher education institutions, private companies, public bodies and other agencies.

2   The linkages that the schools made with their external stakeholders became more sophisticated. Once the journey had started and change had been initiated, it was not sufficient simply to communicate with those in the school's environment and to make them welcome. Nor was it now appropriate to use the various agencies in the school's environment simply to assist the change processes in the school. The emphasis shifted to the creation of productive relationships. Those in the school's wider community were asked to contribute to the school's work and to add value to the school's own endeavours.

3   As the schools changed, there were clear indications that they were managing their boundaries proactively. The development of appropriate

relationships with the wider community became a management task. This management task became more widely owned as links with the wider community came increasingly from a larger number of locations and levels in the school. For example, a range of teachers and heads of department became involved in the transfer of pupils between schools, in order to enhance curriculum continuity. This increasing sophistication in boundary management was continued in the post-acceleration stage.

In this acceleration stage, the focus of attention on teaching and learning sharpened. There were indications that the focus in this stage was beginning to be on *improving* the teaching and learning process. The shift was one from ensuring that the primary tasks of teaching and learning were carried out, to improving the way in which those primary tasks were carried out. So for example, there was a shift towards pupil involvement in learning and developing new learning strategies. A leadership task for the teaching staff was to enable the pupils to take up, engage with and enact their role as learners. The pupils were encouraged to change their view of learning and how they were involved in the learning process. This change of role represented a transformation in the learners' role. The quality of teaching and learning was evaluated; there appeared to be a commitment to professional development and its effective management to improve teaching and learning.

Although there was a sense in which schools in an acceleration stage were simply carrying on with what was started as they moved out of the static and ineffective pre-acceleration stage, the political climate for change was different. For the headteachers, they were now leading in a climate of change for improvement, and within this climate of change, they were experiencing enhanced leadership authority. Their power was evident in what was discussed in the school and what was not. The discourse in the school became more focused on the system's primary tasks of teaching and learning. In terms of the basic tendencies of groups, the school as a group was focusing more on its primary task. This was able to happen because the leadership was containing the emotions and anxieties associated with the primary tasks and with the dismantling of social defences against the primary task. Those taken-for-granted manifestations of power, for example 'It's not worth attempting to teach well, there's no point', had been confronted and were being overcome. In the changed environment for teaching and learning, for example, the icons of leadership power were beginning to be evident.

8 Going strategic

The post-acceleration stage

Introduction

The acceleration phase described in the previous chapter set in motion a large number of changes designed to improve pupil achievement. However, from our conversations with those working in these improved schools, the period of acceleration was not sustained, nor probably was it sustainable. It appeared to be a transitory phase through which many of the schools passed on the way to a culture of sustained and systematic improvement. There appeared to be a variety of explanations for the transient nature of the acceleration phase. First, many of the changes put into place became embedded into the fabric of the 'new' school. That is, those changes that had been put in place became part of the new culture. Second, the climate of change that had been created was perhaps unsustainable. The energy put into the system, the number of changes set in train, and the range of initiatives could not be continued at the same pace. Third, there is also an argument that the acceleration phase should not be sustained. It had served its purpose in enabling the institution to learn to change and to live with change.

The next phase of the journey was qualitatively different from the acceleration phase. This chapter explores some of the themes that emerged in the data that characterised this post-acceleration stage. As with the previous chapters that have described the improvement journey, there is a section at the end that seeks to make sense of events and processes that characterise this stage.

The post-acceleration phase

As with change in any organisation, there is a danger that having achieved significant improvement, schools may return to their former 'non-moving' status, albeit performing at a higher level than before. As Stoll and Fink (1996) make clear, 'The most challenging aspect of leading moving schools is to maintain the momentum.' For the schools coming to the end of the acceleration stage, the challenge appeared to have two dimensions. First, there was a need to ensure that the reflective and adaptive capabilities, which had been developed and secured during the acceleration phase were not lost. Retaining these capabilities would ensure that the school remained an improving school. Second, there was a need to embed the changes that had been achieved in a new culture. This dimension of the challenge is primarily about ensuring effectiveness. Ensuring effectiveness would make sure that the school remained an improved school. Responding to these two challenges is an important leadership task, as we discuss in Chapter 9.

Many of the schools entering and progressing in a post-acceleration phase were, as far as we could ascertain, qualitatively different from those which we might consider as accelerating schools. From our data, there was evidence that many of the schools were developing a strong sense of purpose, realistic expectations and a commitment to learners, their families and communities. These schools were characterised by a continued focus on systematic and sustained change to whole-school and classroom practices in order to enhance pupil achievement. In a successful post-acceleration phase, there was also evidence that management and leadership were increasingly assertive and strategic, hence the description, 'Going strategic' in the chapter heading. Operating in the post-acceleration phase was not easy, and many headteachers highlighted the difficulties and the new challenges they faced in maintaining the momentum for improvement.

The schools in this phase displayed a number of different features, and a number of themes appeared to be significant.

Re-creating the 'new'

In many instances in this stage, the headteachers appeared to have adapted their leadership style in a way that we have described as 're-creating the new'. In this process, the headteachers (and now the wider leadership in the school) were able to find fresh challenges for the staff (and themselves), to generate further improvements, identify new points of leverage for improvement, and to learn from and adapt ideas from elsewhere. In a sense, the leaders were able periodically to reposition themselves as leaders and take a new approach. The practice was an essential part of the move from problem solving (a characteristic of leadership as schools move out of the pre-acceleration phase) into a problem-seeking and solving mode, a characteristic of schools in the post-acceleration and improvement phase. It was also a question of adopting a new leadership style and approach, and being continuously ready to do so. The headteacher of a school which had previously been on the verge of failing indicated that:

> The ethos of this school is *now* one of striving for continuous improvement – staff share the vision. The first phase of improvement

was relatively easy; it is the next stage which will be difficult as expectations have been raised all around. Nothing we have ever tried to do here has collapsed. There is nothing that we have attempted that has broken down. We have tinkered. We have adjusted and said that next time we could do it a little bit better. But nothing has failed. We will go on developing new ideas. We will continue to strive for improvement. You can never rest on your laurels. There is always something else. The world changes. You have got to adjust and adapt too.

Continuing to empower staff

The change in leadership behaviour often led to enhanced autonomy among the teaching staff. Heads of department in secondary schools and curriculum co-ordinators in primary schools took on an increasingly large share of the leadership role. In a sense, they began to take charge of change. As the improvement process moved closer to the classroom, the school's capacity for change increased. This movement of the location of leadership into the organisation, and the accompanying benefits, are well established in the literature on leadership.

In primary schools, where curriculum co-ordinators had been empowered to become leaders and to play a leadership role in improving classroom practice, the headteacher's role changed significantly. One headteacher reported that: 'There were times when I felt redundant! I gave them the power to develop themselves in that role and I can't criticise them for that or take it away now.' In practice, however, this headteacher had not relinquished authority, as conversations with his staff confirmed. His sense of redundancy came from an impression that his former leadership approach of being the single heroic leader responsible for initiating and carrying through all change was no longer appropriate. He needed to adapt his style as the support he had given his staff to act with greater autonomy – and the opportunities he had given them – took effect.

Clarifying the systems

In many cases, the roles and responsibilities of individual members of staff became even more clearly defined. In this new way of working, the collaborative, team-based culture appeared to strengthen, and teams continued to work closely together. In some instances, the teams were given increasing autonomy in determining the strategies they used to reach their targets. In a small number of cases, improvement 'teams', including pupils and parents, were used to investigate and suggest improvements for specific aspects of provision. In these cases, the outcomes of the projects provided the management of the school with valuable feedback. The level of autonomy in such schools often appeared to be considerable, as the teaching and ancillary staff gained in confidence, developed their self-esteem, and acquired new skills and professional expertise. The problem-solving approach adopted by these schools appeared to be well developed, and there was growing emphasis on the importance of enquiry and analytical reflection. In highlighting the importance of these developments, the headteacher of one of the secondary schools explained:

> Self-managing teams have been developed which, within agreed school policies, define their own working practices, set their own targets, give their own spin to the strategies, define excellence in their own faculty teams and measure themselves against it.

One primary school headteacher, commenting on how staff had developed and the school improved significantly, said that:

> These are very good staff. They are not parochial. Not insular. Neither are they constantly looking out for themselves. They are very sharing of resources, of time. There is a lot of co-operation here. People shoulder their responsibilities without being asked. Staff help each other. You couldn't put a price on it. The team work together. There is very close liaison. This is a staff who are full of ideas – all of the time. Especially if it's a passion of theirs in a particular subject or co-ordinating area.

Involving the whole school in strategic management

As the schools made their way along the pathway, the teaching staff appeared to become more involved in strategic planning. School and increasingly departmental development planning became more refined and detailed. In the more sophisticated examples, members of staff understood, were involved in and had a sense of ownership of the planning process. Once development priorities had been identified, school goals were translated into targets (that were measurable in some sense) along with the strategies to achieve them. Typically, a limited number of very specific targets were set which included quantitative and qualitative success criteria. The use of process and outcome targets for improvement was more widespread. Process targets focused on a change in development or policy and practice relating to the school's teaching or organisation. From development plans, outcome targets focusing on pupils' attainment were expressed in a variety of ways. Each target was accurately costed and realistic timescales for achievement established. Resource and training implications were identified. Responsibility for the achievement of specific targets was allocated to named members of staff.

Focusing on the primary task: the improvement of teaching and learning.

During this phase, there appeared to be a continual and strong focus on the processes of teaching and learning, with a clear emphasis on improving educational achievement. Monitoring and evaluation of school and pupil performance typically became more sophisticated and rigorous. During the interviews, many headteachers talked about the importance of using data, and of using it to better effect and for the benefit of pupils. One headteacher referred to this process as the school becoming 'information rich'. The collection of data on school and pupil performance was more comprehensive and, importantly, more systematic than in the past. The information generated was analysed rigorously to identify areas of underachievement that needed to be addressed at whole school, subject, classroom and individual pupil levels.

Although some secondary schools had made a conscious decision not to formally assess pupils on entry, there was an increasing interest in the use of data on pupils' prior attainment as measured by, for example, the NFER Cognitive Abilities Test scores. Rigorous analysis of data assisted schools in the identification of achievement or under-achievement, and enabled the schools to put in place a wide range of strategies to address these issues and support pupils.

Many of the schools used an increasingly wide variety of monitoring activities, for example, 'pupil pursuit', more focused sampling of pupils' work, and monitoring of specific aspects of provision. In a number of cases, guidelines and operating procedures were agreed in advance for the introduction of peer observation. Consultation with the staff had been an important feature of this implementation and typically, all members of staff were monitored including the headteacher. While instant feedback to individual members of staff was not always possible, the outcomes of monitoring were shared with staff. The professional discourse in the school was thereby enhanced, with the dissemination of best practice given a high priority. In many cases, the outcomes were published in in-house documents which were circulated to all departments for further detailed discussion. Those we spoke to who used this approach considered that the dissemination needed to be handled sensitively. Some reported that problems can arise when one department or section of a school is significantly more effective that others and is used as a model for others to copy. In a number of schools, members of the teaching staff increasingly engaged in reflection and enquiry as they continued to focus on improving the quality of teaching and learning, which were now clearly identified as the core functions of the school.

Managing human resources strategically

Successful schools in this post-acceleration phase recognised that the recruitment, selection and induction procedures, professional development and career planning for the members of the teaching staff had to become more sophisticated if they were to continue to move along the improvement pathway. Recruitment processes in some instances involved applicants in a discussion on lesson plans that they had prepared in advance of interview. In some cases, applicants were required to spend a period of time in classrooms and in discussion with other members of staff on the day of interview. The induction procedures for successful applicants were increasingly rigorous and carefully planned to ensure that new members of staff were familiar with school policies and procedures. To meet objectives, training needs were identified through the school development plan, and training was provided both within the schools and by external providers. Ongoing professional development to meet the career needs and aspirations of individual members of staff was also given a high priority. In many schools, all staff who participated in courses were required to produce oral and written reports to their departments or teams, and written reports to the management of the school. In these reports the teachers were required to include information on how the training would be used to impact on pupils' experiences. Reflecting the views of senior staff in many of the schools, one secondary school headteacher indicated that:

> The subject knowledge and personal and professional skills of staff need to be continuously updated; when skills become obsolete, retraining needs to be provided. Management needs to create a working environment where the emphasis is on quality and continuous improvement. Staff motivation needs to be high. Staff need to be clear about the goals of the organisation so that there may be planned progress about what is required from them and to know that action within these guidelines will be supported and encouraged.

The schools also showed increasing interest in the devices used by industrial/commercial organisations to improve quality, particularly those where the focus was on the development of human resources, for example, Total Quality Management programmes. In some instances, external consultants were used to develop staff expertise in areas such as quality assurance, leadership and team building. The benefits were highlighted by one primary headteacher:

> I was with people from industry. I hadn't had much opportunity to meet with people from other walks of life. What came over me was that there are certain skills that you need to develop if you are in a position of leadership. It took the blinkers off a little bit. Working with people outside of education was stimulating.

Promoting pupils' self-esteem/self-confidence

The importance of good relationships between staff and pupils was widely accepted, as was the major impact these relationships can have on the quality of learning. Typically, strategies to promote the self-esteem and the confidence of pupils were constantly under review, and a number of schools implemented particular programmes such as schemes rewarding good work and behaviour or improvement. For example, evidence from an inspection report of one school found that its Positive Discipline programme designed to reinforce good behaviour in and out of the classroom and a positive work ethic was 'a powerful means of promoting pupils' social development'. The programme had established clear and high expectations in terms of behaviour and work. It involved pupils and parents. The pupils and their parents were provided with written guidelines which set out what pupils had to do, and the framework in which they were to do it. Performance in these areas was assessed weekly, and progress tracked using a detailed and clearly structured system which was monitored by senior staff. The programme was well understood by pupils, and it contributed significantly to the development of self-discipline, as it was the pupils' own actions that triggered rewards and sanctions. Pupils knew that there was a clear connection between their behaviour, attitude to work and performance. A wide range of rewards, including trips abroad and participation in 'master classes' played an important role in motivating pupils. Where there was cause for concern, follow-up action was taken and parents were informed.

In many schools, participation in a wide range of extra-curricular activities, including residential and workplace experiences, also contributed significantly to raising pupils' self-esteem and confidence. Their achievements in these activities were also included in their Record of Achievement portfolios. Recognition and appreciation of the efforts made by staff and of their contribution to pupils' successes were also considered important.

Communication of achievements

Improvements in practice and the achievements of pupils were communicated regularly and frequently. Photographs of successful pupils, trophies, awards, letters of commendation, were often prominently displayed in public areas of the school. Other strategies to publicise the pupils' achievements included the use of newsletters, school brochures and regular publication of articles about the school and pupils' achievements in the local press. This communication was seen as part of an overall approach aimed at raising expectations. In the words of one secondary school headteacher:

> The pupils are much more aware than in the past about the need to raise standards. There is a different atmosphere in the classrooms and around the school. They are much more aware of what they are really here for, and of the importance of raising achievements. They are aware of how we focus on those who are achieving well. We congratulate them and their parents. They are also aware of how we pick up

those who are under-achieving. They know that the school is concerned about their progress. Pupils know that if they start to slide that it is only a matter of time before someone comes along and says, look, we expect better of you. They know that our expectations of them are high. They are reminded of this at every opportunity.

The importance of information

Successful 'post-acceleration' schools clearly recognised the importance of information and being 'information rich'. Information in this context means not only data about pupil performance, but also data about other aspects of the school. Schools were aware of the information they needed, had strategies in place to collect information, and knew how to use the knowledge they acquired. They listened to and importantly, heard the 'voices' of pupils, parents and staff. They also collected material about the ways in which the school was functioning well and the ways in which it was not working well.

A minority of schools used formal surveys and questionnaires to determine the views of pupils, staff and parents on whole-school and classroom issues and on school performance. Where opinions were sought, the schools gained useful insight and information on important aspects of the school's work. For example, in one school a survey of members of staff indicated that while they had a very clear view of the way forward and the part they had to play, they thought that the senior management was less inclined than previously to listen to their views. This state of affairs was beginning to affect morale and motivation.

Surveys of parents also helped to highlight differences between the views of parents in different year groups, or between the parents of boys and girls. Where there were matters of real concern, working groups or improvement teams involving parents, staff and pupils were set up to decide how to overcome the problem and set targets for the implementation of measures. Members of staff leading such project groups were often involved in monitoring the implementation of the improvement strategies the groups had developed. This approach was a useful mechanism for involving a wider range of staff in the full process of improvement and the concept of monitoring provision, in some instances across the whole school. A headteacher indicated that 'Improvement teams are part of the continuous need to keep things going; to prevent things from going stale.'

One secondary school had established a monthly parents' clinic where parents could call on a 'drop-in' basis to discuss any issue of interest or concern. This strategy was useful for finding out the views of parents and for involving them in their children's education. The headteacher of the school outlined the benefits of the scheme:

At the monthly clinics the parents come and talk to us about any matter that concerns them. The clinic also gives us an opportunity to ask particular parents to come in and talk to us about their child. The clinics are exceedingly well attended. The senior management team are in the school from 3.15 p.m. for as long as it takes to see the parents. Sometimes it's after 7 p.m.: It has been very valuable and appreciated by parents who don't finish work until 5 p.m. We have learnt a lot about what parents are thinking. They are able to talk to us about any problems that they might be facing. Sometimes these relate directly to their child and school. Other problems might be personal, such as family separations or financial problems which can affect their child. I would strongly recommend it.

Parental and community involvement in the work of the school

As schools continued on their journey of improvement, effective relationships and partnerships were developed further not only with pupils but also with parents, governors and the wider community. Parents and other visitors were actively welcomed to the school. While it would be inaccurate to infer that all teachers felt comfortable with the idea of parental involvement in the classroom itself, the staff in many schools become increasingly confident in involving and working with parents. For example, in many infant, junior and primary schools and in a small number of secondary schools, parents were involved regularly in the classroom, where they provided the teachers with invaluable support. The parents also benefited as they not only participated in enjoyable and rewarding experiences but also had opportunities to develop themselves, and to gain tangible benefits from their experiences. For example, in one infant school, some of the original members of the group of parents who helped in the classroom (the group was nicely named the 'Helping Hands' group) had progressed to paid employment as teachers' aides. In an area of high unemployment, initiatives such as these provided very valuable job opportunities, particularly where there was some formal recognition or accreditation of their work with children. One teacher's aide was very enthusiastic about her involvement with the school and how it had helped her:

> I was a 'Helping Hand' for some time before I became a teacher's aide; this really helped me to build up my self-confidence. It can be very isolated living in this community once the children are at school. I love it here (in school). It's brilliant. I've learnt so much that not only helps me here but also with my own children.

In some schools, home–school contracts had been developed to formalise the partnership between the families and the school. These set out the obligations in the home–school partnership clearly and gave a guarantee of what the school promised to do and what the school asked of parents. Many infant and primary schools had also developed innovative programmes of tasks for the pupils to complete at home. These tasks, which were used to foster discussions and written work, often contributed significantly to pupils' learning. They also helped to improve communication with parents about the work of the school. For schools securely operating in a successful post-acceleration period, there was a greater sense of mutual confidence between the schools and the communities that the schools served. In many of these schools, the number of pupils on the roll had increased, and parents went to considerable trouble to transport their children to a particular school.

In many schools, links with the governing body were now well developed, very effective and valued by all of those involved. The head-teachers actively encouraged governors to become involved in the life of the school and to develop a greater understanding of how the school operated, at both whole-school and individual classroom levels. Maximum use was made of the expertise of governors as schools continued to move forward, and they were closely involved with staff in setting realistic and manageable targets for improvement.

Widening horizons and extending the network

An important change in the 'mind-sets' of the schools in this phase was a desire to widen the perspective of all those in the school and to participate in a much wider network of schools and communities. Many respondents talked about the need to 'widen horizons'. The following quote illustrates this point well:

> There are many good things one can associate with a valley, with a Welsh valley in particular. Things like the closeness of the community, the warmth of the people. But, valleys as geographical features have somewhat limited horizons. They are often containers rather than conduits. So one of the challenges that faced this school was to look outwards in all sorts of ways. Out to our local community. Out beyond our local community. Out to other schools. And, through our infor-mation technology links to a more cosmopolitan world.

A number of schools, particularly secondary schools, had developed strong links with local industries and the business community. These links benefited pupils and staff, who often gained access to a wider range of specialist expertise and up-to-date technology and equipment. In the view of one headteacher:

> It is very important for the school to have powerful links with industry. For example local engineering firms who are attached to each year group bring expertise into the school and help to set up projects. Some

companies offer training days for our pupils in Years 9 and 10, while others provide training for our staff in quality techniques, leadership and team building.

In another secondary school, members of the local business community were introduced into the daily life of the school through the Personal and Social Education programme, study clubs, and science visits. In addition, forty business 'mentors' from a wide range of organisations engaged with pupils over the age of fourteen. While originally this involvement was intended as preparation for work experience, it was now securely linked with the achievement of various 'Compact' agreements (see Chapter 7). Many of the mentors visited the Year 10 and 11 pupils on work experience, and the pupils benefited from the interest shown by an additional adult who was concerned with their progress.

As they strove for continuous improvement, many schools sought to collaborate with similar schools in an attempt to network, benchmark their activities and to share good practice at whole school and specialist levels. Contact was also made with schools further afield, often resulting in pupil and staff exchanges and participation in joint projects, such as Agenda 21, an initiative for environmental improvement. Schools which were involved in providing placements for initial teacher training reported that members of their teaching staff were becoming more reflective on their own practice as they observed and supported student teachers. Strong links with higher education providers also helped to raise pupils' expectations and to facilitate transition.

In a number of schools, the Internet not only provided access to a wide range of information systems but also enabled staff and pupils to communicate on a regular and frequent basis with schools across the world. For example, many schools involved in the project have set up websites on the Internet. In some cases these were used as an electronic 'prospectus' for the school, while other schools designed the website as a curriculum resource for other schools to use. Where such contacts were effective they made a significant impact on the curriculum and in broadening the horizons of all those involved.

The physical environment

As a school progressed on its journey, the improvement in the school's physical environment often reflected the increased pride and confidence which staff and pupils had in the school. Premises and grounds were cleaner and, where financial resources permitted, were better maintained. In many primary schools, the rather barren playgrounds had been significantly developed into stimulating and attractive areas, often with the help of parents, grandparents and other members of the community. The visitor reception areas in many of the schools were well organised and welcoming. Displays of pupils' work were of a very high standard. Pupils knew that their own teachers and other members of the staff valued their work. The displays were used to support teaching and learning and to make a significant contribution to raising the pupils' self-esteem. For example, in primary schools the attractive and colourful theme displayed in classrooms and corridors created a cheerful, stimulating learning environment which was used to maximum effect to promote and celebrate learning. In secondary schools, increasing emphasis was placed on the importance of display, though in practice its quality was often more variable.

Resources for teaching and learning

A key feature of schools securely in a post-acceleration phase was that teachers had access to good quality resources that supported teaching and learning and which were sufficiently differentiated to meet the individual needs of pupils. Teaching areas were organised and managed to improve the quality and range of pupils' learning. For example, in many of the primary schools, the organisation of the classrooms facilitated the implementation of new initiatives, such as the 'literacy hour' or the 'numeracy hour.' In many secondary schools, classrooms were often grouped as suites of specialist rooms to encourage departmental/faculty team work, to facilitate the sharing of resources which supported teaching and learning. Development of the physical environment also encouraged the use of a wider range of learning activities. In addition to appropriate textbooks and practical materials, pupils were given increasing access to a suitably wide range of other learning resources such as audio-visual facilities, classroom computers, information technology suites, upgraded libraries and/or Learning Resource Centres. In secondary schools, learning resources typically reflected current business practice, for example, for General National Vocational Qualifications (GNVQ) programmes. Where enterprising headteachers had raised additional funds through their links with industry and commerce both locally and nationally, these were frequently used to provide additional equipment and resources.

Some interpretation and sense-making

We have termed this phase 'going strategic' in an attempt to capture the nature of the schools in this position as we experienced them. As in previous chapters, which have described the different stages in the journey, this final section of the chapter attempts briefly to make sense of these characteristics and their purpose from the institutional transformation perspective.

'Recreating the new' was a significant theme in this stage. This process or leadership strategy appears to be an attempt to recapture the essence of the fracturing of the culture which, in so many of the schools we studied, initiated the improvement journey. One of the problems facing head-teachers (and for that matter, leaders of any organisation) is that they become trapped in their own patterns of action, their typical responses to situations and their preferences, both their likes and dislikes. These are in part shaped by their own predispositions, principles, values and beliefs. But they are also significantly formed by the expectations and emotional projections of others. These projections may see the leader as a 'knight in shining armour' who will save the school, or the leader may well be seen as a destructive figure who will do the school great harm. The leader may attract powerful unconscious projections which might include envy, loathing, devotion, fondness, rivalry and distaste. Over time these influences can be constraining, entrapping and limiting. The projections can be particularly difficult to cope with because they are likely to be made by the 'followers' and received by the 'leaders' unconsciously. They restrict the potential for change and adaptation that is essential for effective and appropriate contingent leadership action. It is necessary for leaders to 're-create the new' so that they and their followers do not become immobilised by their own expectations of themselves and the projections and expectations of others. Leaders and followers must have the capacity to change lest they fall foul of the paralysing effects of such projections and expectations, and lose sight of their own potential for individuation, their own diversity and their particular desires. For leaders, re-creating the new achieves this outcome. In essence it regenerates leadership authority.

In terms of interpreting the characteristics of this phase, again many of the themes evident earlier in the journey were sustained and continued. The continuing efforts to empower the staff meant that in some instances the headteacher's role at an operational level had to change. In these cases, the headteacher's role in the detailed working of the school was no longer as significant, and the role had to be adapted substantially in response to empowered members of staff fully taking up their own roles. Including the whole school staff in strategic management extended their involvement in whole school planning. It also further developed collaboration in the school, again with all the explanations, interpretations and purposes that such a collaborative approach carries (see Chapter 6). At this stage of the journey, the notion of staff/professional development was extended to encompass the effective management of all the human resources in the school at every stage from the identification of staffing needs, through recruitment and selection, to induction, development and career progression. The promotion of pupil esteem and self-confidence became more sophisticated and in support of the primary task of teaching and learning. Importantly, there were attempts to transform the way in which learners view their task and engage in it.

In this post-acceleration phase, there no longer appeared to be a need to celebrate achievements in order to inject high levels of positive feedback into the system. Achievements were communicated to ensure that feedback was returned to the system, but the communication process was more part of a strategic process of informing key stakeholders. Relationships with those who had an interest in and were of interest to the schools became more sophisticated in this phase. To summarise the processes typical of this stage.

1   The views of those individuals and agencies in the school's environment are gathered and considered. This process helps to ensure that the school is doing what those key stakeholders require. In a theoretical sense, the collection of information in this way helps to ensure that the primary task of the system is appropriate to the requirements of the environment. This activity is an important aspect of the leadership role.

2   The participation of the community that the school serves in the school's primary tasks – teaching and learning – is extended. The boundary is now managed in such a way as to ensure that involvement of others from the school's environment is both extensive and appropriate.

3   There are further and wider linkages with the wider environment beyond the immediate environs of the school.

4   The school uses information to ensure that it is meeting the needs of key stakeholders both within and outside the institution. It is aware of the information it needs, knows how to acquire the information, and how to use the information it has acquired.

The management of relationships with key stakeholders in the school's external environment becomes a key management task. The leadership role with those key stakeholders is also important and is discussed in Chapter 9.

Resources to assist with the primary tasks of teaching and learning are managed, as is the physical environment of the school. Interestingly and significantly, the primary task changes and extends. It moves clearly from carrying out the tasks of teaching and learning to *improving* the ways in which the tasks of teaching and learning are carried out. This shift requires a change in the way in which the teachers view their role. The main change is that the teachers fully take up, engage with and enact their role. They are clear about its contribution to the whole institution, and they see its inter-relationship with the roles of other teachers in the school. Their view of their role is dynamic, and they have the capacity to consider their role reflectively and reflexively so that they can adapt it and improve it. For the learners, their role may also be transformed. They move from a position where they are fixed in a role which has little meaning or purpose and where they are passive. In that position, they have not fully taken up, engaged with and enacted their role as learners. As their view of their role is transformed, they move to a position where they are active participants as learners and purposefully take up, engage with and enact the role of learner.

This transformation in many ways represents an end-point to the journey of improvement and educational transformation. At this point, the school has adapted itself so that teaching and learning take place effectively and are continuously improving. Of course, the notion of a 'journey's end' is illusory, in that there are always changes and improvements to be made. It does however represent a new way of 'being' in the school. That is why the term 'institutional transformation' or 'educational transformation' is appropriate. Leadership in this transformation process is significant and is dealt with in the next chapter.

9 The leadership of educational transformation

Introduction

Many of the schools we visited during this study had undergone considerable change. Some of those had undergone radical change. A number of those we studied in detail as case studies had been transformed from being schools that were incapable of change and ineffective (certainly in simple process and output terms) to those that were capable of change and effective. This change represents a transformation. While a number of themes emerged from the data, a key determinant, if not *the* key factor in accelerating the performance of schools, appeared to be the quality of the leadership in the schools. Often, and especially so in the initiation of the improvement journey, that leadership was embodied in the *ex officio* leader, the headteacher.

This chapter explores some of the issues in leadership in the process of educational transformation. First, there is a section that briefly addresses the assumption that the quality of the *ex officio* leader, the headteacher, is the main determinant of effectiveness and improvement in schools. There is then a section that summarises some of the characteristics of leadership as revealed by the study. The third section entitled 'The leadership principles' attempts to capture the essence of leadership. The early part of this section rehearses the most important aspects of what we know about leadership that might inform a consideration of how leadership should be. The remainder of the section outlines the leadership principles themselves.

A note of caution about leaders and change

It is very difficult to establish which particular change or essential ingredient results in an improvement in pupil achievement. The schools we looked at in the study presented us with an immense amount of data about the changes that had taken place in their improvement journeys. In Chapter 2 we listed what the schools had achieved in terms of the detailed modifications they had made to bring about improvement in the achievements of their pupils. The problem is that schools are complex systems and it is often difficult to say unequivocally that a change in the process – one specific change or one deliberate action or one particular event – is the cause of change in the output of the system. For most changes, there are just far too many intervening variables to establish that causal link.

Despite the difficulty of establishing clear linkages between particular phenomena and improvement, one consistent factor in all the schools appeared to be leadership. Typically the headteacher, certainly in the early stages of the improvement journey, was the expression of that leadership. It seemed that the headteacher had a key role in initiating the change, sustaining it and managing it.

Although we believe that effective leadership is essential in change in schools, a little caution needs to be exercised in asserting that view. First, there is a seductive assumption that if change has occurred, it must have been led. In attempting to identify the essence of that leadership, understandably, one first looks to the headteacher. It is then easy to assume that if the change has been successful it must have been led successfully, and that we can attribute this successful leadership to the headteacher. However, change is complex and change in schools is particularly complicated. The interplay between leadership and the initial conditions, the initiation of change, the institution's change capability and the purpose of change, all play a part in the change process. We visited schools where enormous change had taken place but where it was clear, often from the accounts of the headteachers themselves, that the starting conditions were right and that the school was ready for change. In these situations the leadership task, though still daunting and challenging, had been more straightforward than in other settings. As a result, progress had been more substantial and the leader's perceived capability and reputation was high. However, a different picture emerges if that leadership effort is contrasted with the leadership efforts of a headteacher where the initial conditions were unfavourable and the school's ability to change was limited. Here the leadership task would have been more difficult, the progress of change slower and the leader's perceived capability and reputation would have been lower as a result. In straightforward terms, is the leader's task one of simply lighting the blue touch paper and watching as the rocket takes off, or does the leader have to build the rocket from scratch in the rain? A further complication is that luck and chance can also play a key part in the change process. At best, all we can say is that the leadership capability of the headteacher is probably important and necessary but on its own is unlikely to be sufficient to bring about institutional change and improvement. If we accept that assertion, what were the characteristics of successful leadership demonstrated by those in our study?

Some leadership characteristics

Perhaps unsurprisingly, the characteristics of leadership of educational change which the study revealed were numerous. In the schools where the change had been successful and substantial, the characteristics were personified in the headteacher, but as the change journey unfolded, others increasingly took up leadership roles. It seems that leadership moved from the *ex officio* leader to others in the school. In essence, those in leadership positions and exercising leadership in the school appeared to exhibit the following characteristics.

- An ability to analyse the strengths and weaknesses of the school and to convince staff, governors, parents and pupils that change and improvement are necessary and achievable.
- A clear perception of the individuality of the school, its unique features and the particular qualities of the community it serves.
- A clear vision of long-term goals and the ability to select strategic priorities for change and improvement.
- Knowing how to create a climate in which change for improvement can take place.
- The skills to manage people and the courage and determination to deal with difficult situations.
- A willingness and ability to alter management systems in order to facilitate change and establish clearly defined accountabilities.
- An understanding of the central importance of change and improvement to the core functions of the school, teaching and learning.
- A commitment to supporting the professional development of staff so that they become the main agents of change.
- The ability to inspire, motivate and engage with staff at a range of levels from the personal to the professional.
- The ability to delegate and to inspire others to take on leadership roles.
- The ability to integrate the various functions of the school to create a unified school with a strong sense of purpose.
- The ability to control the pace of change so that progress is sustained, incremental and becomes integrated into the school's life and work.

In a sense, this list is what one might expect from an analysis of the characteristics of successful leaders. A key question remains: 'Can further sense be made of such characteristics together with what we know of leadership from the literature in order to draw up a set of useful leadership principles?' And beyond that: 'Is there any further theorisation which might prove helpful in understanding leadership and in providing a helpful basis for appropriate leadership action?'

A set of principles for school leadership

This section sets out some principles that could usefully underpin effective leadership in schools. There are four sub-sections. The first examines some general considerations of leadership. The second looks at the leadership purpose. Without an understanding of purpose it is impossible to make much sense of leadership actions. The third section outlines a set of leadership principles on which effective leadership action can be based and considered. The final sub-section selects some of the principles from this study that seem to capture the essence of leadership for educational change.

Some general considerations

This short section sets out some general considerations that help to lay a foundation for a set of leadership principles.

Leadership can operate at different levels

The issue of levels of leadership has been reviewed in Chapter 3. To rehearse the main issue: although leadership is often described in terms of the leader of an institution, such a conceptualisation is quite a narrow one. Leadership can operate at a number of levels. These levels include the following.

- *Self-leadership*. At this level, leadership is concerned with a set of strategies that individuals use to influence and to improve their own behaviours.
- *Leadership of individual others*. Leadership at this level involves two participants, the leader and another. Mentoring, role modelling, advocacy, supervision and coaching would, for example, come under this heading. Arguably, these are very significant leadership activities but are relatively under-valued in terms of their potential contribution to change management and leadership. The leadership role in such relationships may be defined, perhaps hierarchically, but not necessarily so. The leadership role may also change in such relationships.
- *Leadership of small groups and teams*. This level of leadership would typically involve leading a relatively permanent sub-unit of the whole system such as a department in a secondary school. But it might also involve leading a temporary, *ad hoc* group that has a specific organisational task or problem to solve. It could entail adopting a leadership role, perhaps temporarily, in a self-managed group. Working at this level, the leader has to engage with the dynamics and default tendencies of the group.
- *Leadership of the whole institution or strategic leadership*. This level of leadership is the one with which the literature on leadership appears to be most concerned. Paradoxically, it is at this level that the significance of the individual leader for organisational effectiveness and development appears most open to question. Similarly, the validity of the single heroic leader as the main approach to organisational leadership

has been questioned. The executive team, or senior management group, where the leadership of the institution is shared, has been offered as a more productive alternative. Although monitoring the environment and strategy formulation in relation to the environment features in the leadership literature, the notion of the leadership of an institution's environment is relatively under-developed as an idea. This leadership of the key stakeholders in the institution's environment is important for two reasons. First, leadership, conceptualised as enabling others to take up and enact a role, would appear to be crucial in collaborative and partnership-based activities with other institutions. Second, leadership of the key stakeholders in the institution's environment is particularly significant in educational institutions. For a school, the development of productive and supportive relationships with those in the institution's environment, such as parents and the wider community, is crucial. The development of a shared understanding of the school's aims and purposes with those stakeholders is equally fundamental.

From our research, it was clear that many of those who were in leadership positions were capable of leading at a variety of levels in their schools. Those who were effective as leaders conveyed a strong sense of their own personal mission, formed positive relationships with other individuals, led their own institution effectively and formed effective 'leaderly' relationships with those in their school's environment.

Management, leadership and administration overlap and are interrelated

Any set of leadership principles must recognise the overlap and interrelationship between management, leadership and administration. It is of course interesting to attempt to distinguish between managing, administering and leading. However, what we are concerned with is the practice of organising in schools. That practice can be called management, leadership or administration. It seems that in Britain at least the term 'leadership' is becoming the most widely used term to describe that practice of organising in schools. A central characteristic of the schools we studied was their organising capability. This capability embraced a range of different actions and activities.

Power and influence are central in leadership

Although power and influence are highly problematic notions, they are central in the process of leadership. It is difficult to conceive of leadership without the use of power to influence individuals and events. The issues of power and influence were reviewed in Chapter 4. Three points need to be reasserted here.

1   Power and its use to influence take a number of different forms.
2   Power cycles back and forth between and among individuals and groups in an institution.
3   Only rarely does power flow consistently in one direction in organisations.

Leadership, the management of change and learning are very closely interrelated

As we discussed in Chapter 3, for individuals and organisations to change they must learn to do things differently. Leadership and management of change are centrally concerned with the management of learning in individuals and in the organisation. Those in leadership positions in the schools we studied clearly felt they had a role in the development and education of all those in their schools. For them learning and leadership were closely linked.

Different leadership styles, kinds of leadership and approaches to leadership are of value, but the consistent use of one style of leadership is ultimately limiting

Any set of leadership principles will only be helpful if they allow space for the use of different styles of leadership such as consultative and autocratic styles, shared leadership styles and participative styles. A set of principles should also give space for different kinds of leadership, such as transactional and transformational leadership, and other models of leadership, especially those espoused in educational settings, for example invitational leadership. A framework of principles should not advocate a particular leadership ideology – the one-way model – because such ideologies are ultimately flawed. In the end, they are all undone by the situational and contextualised nature of appropriate leadership. Good leadership is primarily about taking the most appropriate action in any situation. Leadership ideologies constrain this flexibility. Further, as we discussed in Chapter 3, if leadership's primary purpose is to bring about change, then leadership actions must continually be reconfigured in response to the change that the leadership action has itself brought about. The use of varied leadership styles and strategies was a particular feature of those in leadership positions in the schools that we studied. As we have discussed in Chapter 6, approaches to leadership varied from moment to moment and over time.

Effective leadership must be a form of reflexive reflective practice

It was Donald Schon who first used the term 'reflective practice' to explain how professional practitioners think in action (Schon 1983). Reflective practice provides an explanation for the way in which professional practitioners, for example teachers and managers, cope with the diverse, immediate, idiosyncratic, unpredictable, multifaceted and contextual nature of their work. In their practice, professionals are metaphorically in conversation with the context in which they are acting, researching it and acting on the basis of the outcomes of those processes. They are engaged in a process of reflection *in* action. At times outside those of professional action, they reflect *on* their practice (reflection *on* action) in order to learn from it and thereby improve what they do. The reflective processes can occur at the individual, group and whole institution level. Implicit in reflective practice is reflexivity, which enables individuals, groups and institutions to consider what they know in order to scrutinise its validity critically. This reflexivity facilitates a critical examination of rationales for action, values and beliefs. Reflexive reflective practice is important in leadership because any leadership act changes the context for leadership action. It enables the leader continually to act appropriately in a context of change.

Those leaders to whom we spoke were clearly able to reflect on their leadership actions. The varied and contingent nature of their leadership was testimony to their capability to reflect in action. They had a capacity to reflect critically on the way in which their leadership actions related to their professional values and beliefs.

The emotional aspects of leadership action and responses to leadership are fundamental

In this text, we have analysed the management of change from a perspective that has been grounded in the emotional influences on both leadership action and the responses to leadership. Although there may be a surface rationality to leadership and the management of change, there are important emotional dimensions to leadership. Responses to change may be influenced by very powerful non-rational emotional forces. Any set of leadership principles must be founded on an understanding that the emotional dimension of leadership is crucial.

The leadership purpose

The purpose of an action gives insight into the reason for it and its intentions. Purposes are revealed by 'Why?' questions. Without a sense of the 'Why?' of any leadership or change management action, it is difficult to understand: the content of change (What is being changed?); the context of the change (the 'When?' 'Where?' and 'Who?' of change) and the process of change (the How? of change). It is also difficult to make full sense of the ways in which the content, context and process of change interrelate. Also, a sense of purpose interrelates with the aims and gives a sense of direction and destination to the management of change.

So, what was the overall purpose of changes which the schools we studied appeared to have undergone? From our interpretation, many have undergone a radical change and have effectively been transformed as institutions. As explained in Chapter 3, these institutions have moved from being institutions with low change capability (static) and with inappropriate processes and comparably low pupil achievement (ineffective), to being institutions which have and use their capability to change and improve (changing/improving) and have appropriate processes and levels of pupil achievement which compare well with other similar institutions (effective). These changes, in effect, represent an educational transformation. This model gives an insight into the leadership purpose, because the intentions of and reasoning behind the leadership actions were to move the school to the effective and improving position. The educational transformation grid therefore gives an insight into the leadership purpose. Figure 9.1 illustrates the leadership purpose grid.

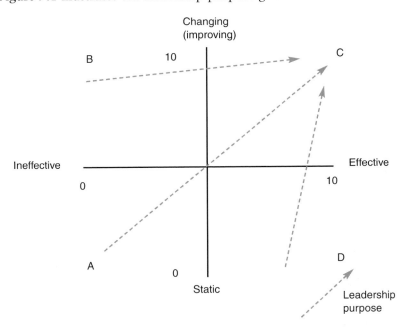

Figure 9.1 The leadership purpose grid

This model raises a number of issues for consideration.

1 The leadership purpose is valid for individual leaders themselves and for leaders in their leadership relationships with individual others, with the institution and the institution's key stakeholders.
2 It could be argued that moving from ineffectiveness to effectiveness is a contractual change, and is therefore a relatively straightforward managerial task. If there are leadership dimensions to ensuring effectiveness they are

limited to those which are largely transactional in nature. The move from static to changing is different. It requires a reconfiguration of the teaching role into one which creates in individuals:

- an enhanced capacity to reflect on their practice with a view to changing and improving it
- a deeper capacity to reflect on their practice in a way which embraces both rational and non-rational dimensions
- an improved capability to reflect constructively on the balance between their own interests and those of the organisation
- a better understanding of the contribution of their role to the organisation's objectives
- a changed perspective on the role which enables individuals to learn through the role and to use it to meet their higher order needs for example, individuation and autonomy
- an understanding that they have a role in enabling others in the organisation to take up and enact their roles
- an enhanced capability to productively adapt their roles to enable the organisation to adapt its processes and purposes.

These changes are immediately recognisable as those associated with transformational leadership.

3   In educational settings, achieving the leadership purpose requires the containment of anxiety, both in the individual leaders and in those being led.

4   All educational organisations will always require leadership for two reasons. First, the measures of effectiveness and improvement on the scales in Figure 9.1 are continually being reset by the demands of the environment and by the institution reflecting on its practices. Second, in schools, leaders have continually and actively to resist the tendency in themselves, in others, in the institution and in the institution's key stakeholders to regress to the static and ineffective position. This regression will be driven by social defences against the anxiety associated with the primary task of enabling learning. Leadership energy is required just to stay in one place!

5   As we discussed in Chapter 3, in education, a change in a school as it journeys from say, A to C in Figure 9.1, has a moral purpose and is at the heart of professional teaching values. Changing a school to ensure that teaching is effective and that the school has the capability to improve that effectiveness represents 'good' change. It is that assertion that makes the leadership of such change 'good' leadership and gives it its moral purpose.

The leadership principles

This section outlines a framework of principles for educational leadership. They embrace the general considerations outlined earlier in the chapter.

They have resulted from a consideration of the meaning of leadership actions identified in the process of school improvement in the schools we studied. We realise that in arriving at these principles we are also drawing on a much wider set of data which includes our own experiences of schools and organising in schools.

In distilling the literature on leadership, our interpretations of leadership in the schools we visited and the purpose of change in schools, we hope we have captured much of the sum and substance of leadership. We recognise that we may be open to criticism because of the easily remembered acronym that these principles give: LEADER. We offer no defence against that criticism except to say that that is how the principles worked out! Yet worse, when we reduce this essence of leadership and leading still further to the key elements we come to the acronym of ERA, again memorable, if only because we seem to be living in an era of leadership in education at the moment (see page 157).

In considering the principles, it needs to be remembered that leadership action through the leadership principles operates at four levels.

1   The leaders themselves.
2   The leaders in relation to others.
3   The leaders in relation to their institutions.
4   The leaders in relation to their institutions' key stakeholders.

The term 'institution' is used here to describe the school as a whole, or any of the constituent parts, such as departments, year-groupings of pupils and form teachers, or senior management teams. Viewing these groupings as systems can help to clarify leadership thinking. It also means that any member of an educational institution can use these principles to think about their own leadership practice. For example, a central part of a teacher's professional autonomy is his or her capability to be self-determining, independent and self-reliant. Teachers need to be able to lead themselves in order to work effectively and, to enhance the effectiveness of the whole institution, to be able to lead others.

The leader as the leading educator

The leading educator role as a part of headship has a long history, and although it has changed somewhat over time it remains valid and important. Being a credible practitioner is important for the authority of educational managers. Usually, for those new to post as, say, a headteacher or a head of department, establishing their own teaching is a prime concern because they see 'being a good teacher' as an important dimension of their leadership and management authority. It is as though being competent and efficient in the classroom gives the new-to-post managers 'ground to stand on' when influencing others with whom they work. But for the purposes of leading in an educational institution, leaders must be the leading educators in two broader senses. First, they have to be experts *in the practice* of learning and development at all levels. That is, they need to be proficient in the practice of developing themselves and others (including developing their institution). Second, as leading educators, they must have expert knowledge *about* learning and development. They need to know about the processes of professional development, career development pathways and likely development needs of individuals. They also need to know about the development of institutions.

THE WORK OF THE LEADING EDUCATOR AT DIFFERENT LEVELS

Being the leader in learning and development means having the expertise to: build learning capability, enhance the motivation to learn, create opportunities to learn and understand the learning purpose in themselves, in others, in their institution and in the institution's key stakeholders. It also means having the expertise and ability to do the following.

- Identify learning 'needs' and to be able to distinguish them from learning 'wants'. For example, a headteacher may feel that what he wants to do is to take a year out on a secondment to industry in order to learn to find out 'how they manage things out there'. The real learning need may be to do with finding ways of coping with the inexorable projections of anxiety from his staff and his inability to deal with them. It is this learning need that makes him want to 'escape' from the school on secondment.
- Understand the context in which learning needs are set. A school may find itself obsessed with competing with its neighbouring school, and consider that its main task is to learn new ways of 'out-doing the opposition'. Its real learning need might be more to do with finding ways of focusing consistently on improving teaching and learning in a careful and thought-through way.
- Grasp the medium and long-term implications of the operation of any strategy implemented to meet learning needs. For example, setting up a school-based management development programme for heads of department in partnership with a local university will inevitably have implications for the school's development programme for a number of years.

The leaders themselves   Leaders should take a leading role in their own development and growth. They must develop their capacity to learn and know, and continually consider their own learning agenda, their development priorities and their learning goals. They need to lead themselves reflectively and reflexively. Although it is possible to undertake self-leadership independently, it is likely to happen best with the support and involvement of others. For many, especially those near to the top of the management hierarchy, engaging the right kind of support can be difficult. This difficulty is exacerbated by the recent trend towards 'flattened hierarchical structures' in many organisations including schools. For headteachers, engaging with the right kind of 'learning partner' can be particularly difficult. The power and authority dimension of the relationships with those to whom they might most readily turn (for example, the chair of governors or the senior staff from the local education authority) will probably disrupt the kind of reflection that an 'other' can engender.

Leaders in relation to others   Leaders should take a leading role in the development and growth of others. This work in leading other individuals can take place through 'formalised' activities and relationships defined variously in the literature as coaching, mentoring, role modelling, advocacy and supervision. However, leading the development and growth of others can be just a part of a normal working relationship. Significant conversations can take place informally, and there is a case for arguing that the leadership of others is best done that way.

In schools, bringing about change in individuals is crucial to institutional change. Because educational change is associated with high levels of anxiety, the leader in the leading educator role will have a role in containing the anxiety associated with undertaking professional learning.

The leaders in relation to their institutions   For the purpose of institutional improvement, it is essential that leaders take the central role in the learning and development of their institutions. This maxim applies to heads of departments, team leaders, and to the leaders of any sub-grouping within the whole institution. Leaders must guide their institution's development as appropriate to its context, set the direction of its development, and know and understand the short, medium and long-term development priorities.

Leaders in relation to their institutions' key stakeholders   Leaders must take on a leading role in the development of others – individuals and organisations – outside the institution who have a stake in their institution, creating developmental relationships and seeking to add value to their own institution through those relationships.

As the leading educators, leaders have to be experts about learning and development. In a sense they have to be the leading 'edge-ucators'. They must have authority in their understanding of change, development and learning. Being the leading educator in a school has an added significance because learning is the institution's primary task. However, it is not sufficient for the headteacher of, for example, a primary school to be an expert in pedagogy. He/she needs to be an expert in working with adult professionals both inside and outside the school and in managing change in the whole institution.

Leadership optimises adaptability

Since leadership is essentially about influencing change, building the capacity to change is crucial. Without change capacity, leadership of an individual or institution cannot take place. Educational leaders have to ensure that they themselves have sufficient capacity for change and have to optimise the capacity for change in others, in the institution as a whole and in the institution's key stakeholders. Broadly, adaptive capacity has three dimensions.

1   *The ability to change.* Without this capability obviously no change can take place either in an individual or an institution.
2   *The motivation to change.* Although an individual or an institution may have the capability to change, they may lack the motivation. If there is no wish or will to change, then no change will take place.
3   *Opportunities to change.* Changing relies on having the opportunity to do so. For those in leadership positions, making opportunities for individuals and the institution to change requires creative thinking and flexibility.

All three dimensions of change capability are expressed in relation to the purpose of change, so a school's adaptive capacity would be the extent to which it can change in order to improve pupil achievement. It will require the ability to improve, the motivation to improve and the opportunities to improve. It is worth stressing the notion of *optimising* adaptability. It is pointless putting energy into enhancing adaptive capability if a higher level of adaptive capability is not required. Some people already have a sufficiently high level. In fact, some people are 'change junkies' and seek change simply as a way of separating themselves from the difficult feelings associated with maintaining the *status quo*. Adaptability is a quality that needs to be optimised rather than continually enhanced.

THE LEADER'S WORK IN OPTIMISING ADAPTABILITY AT THE DIFFERENT LEVELS

The leaders themselves   For the individual leader, adaptability requires the capacity to change moment to moment according to circumstances and over a period of time. The capacity for rapid adaptability is required in order to respond flexibly according to different micro-contexts. For example, working with different colleagues in different situations may demand very different kinds of interaction. The capacity to change over time is also important. Leadership actions have to change in response to the changing and changed culture. It is necessary also to be able to 'recreate the new', a characteristic of many of the headteachers in the study who were successful at managing change over a long period.

The leaders in relation to others   The leader's work with others in optimising adaptability requires encouraging and working with them to build their capability to change, to help them to take risks to be creative, to overcome internal barriers and blockages and, importantly, to enable the individual to live in a changing environment.

The leaders in relation to their institutions   A key task of leadership is to develop and optimise the institution's capacity to change so that improvement can take place.

The leaders in relation to their institutions' key stakeholders   The leader has to develop and optimise the capacity of the institution's key stakeholders to adapt so that they can learn and change.

In a school setting, this capacity building within the institution and with the institution's key stakeholders may involve going through a period of multiple innovation. This period of multiple change enables the school and those who have an interest in it to become used to, and energised by, change. This encouraging of adaptability was one of the purposes of the acceleration period in the schools we studied.

Leadership has 3D vision: determination, direction and destination

The notion of vision is well established in the literature as an important aspect of leadership, and we have looked at the idea of vision and creating a vision in Chapter 3. In educational leadership, vision is important in three particular dimensions: *d*etermination, *d*irection and *d*estination. Hence the notion of '3D vision', another useful acronym.

Determination   is crucial in a number of ways. For individual leaders, determination means having a clear, assured and consistent grasp of their own leadership purpose and consequently the primary task of their leadership in relation to themselves, others, the institution and the institution's key stakeholders.

Direction   is important in two ways.

1   Leaders should know the direction in which the individual leader her/himself, others, and the institution and its key stakeholders should go. The leader has an important role in deciding on the pathway along which the improvement journey will progress. Of course, it is impossible realistically to set the pathway in detail, and it is even undesirable in some ways. There is a good case for letting the strategy emerge as the journey progresses. None the less, setting the direction is a general sense is crucial.

2   The notion of direction is also important in the sense of acting with authority. The idea of the person directing others is often not acceptable: it calls up all sorts of images of bossiness, authoritarianism and dominance. However, acting with authority need not, and indeed should not, be like that. Leaders need some sense of self-direction themselves to ensure that they engage in purposeful leadership action up to the boundaries of their roles. They must also direct others, acting with authority to help and enable them to fulfil their roles effectively. They must use their authority to enable others to act with authority. Leaders also have to direct the institution by establishing and maintaining the systems that enable it to function purposely and effectively and to take up and enact its own role as an institution. Direction for the institutional leader also involves enabling the institution's key stakeholders to fulfil their roles in relation to the institution's purposes.

Destination   entails knowing the 'end point' of the change. What are the leaders trying to achieve for themselves, for others, for the institution as a whole and for the institution's key stakeholders? This notion of 'vision' in leadership is well established in the literature. In radical educational change, articulating the vision to others, the institution and its key stakeholders appears to be very important. Of course, this end point, the destination, is largely illusory and never reached because it is and must be continually re-configured as the institution reflects reflexively on its own 'destination' and in as environmental demands on the school change.

Leadership ensures effectiveness

Educational effectiveness is complicated. There are no easy answers to questions such as: 'What does it mean to be effective as a teacher?' and 'What does it mean for a school to be effective?' But at another level, schools are primarily about enabling learning. The primary task of teachers and schools is to enable the pupils to learn, and it is in that primary task that teachers and schools need to be effective.

The role of leadership in ensuring effectiveness in schools goes beyond simply ensuring that the teaching is effective. That is educational leadership at a transactional, contractual level. Of course, ensuring that kind of effectiveness is important. It will lead to an improvement in pupil achievement. But there is a second dimension that is concerned with being effective in *improving* the way in which the primary task is achieved. This notion is concerned with being effective in improving the processes of teaching and learning, and thereby improving pupil achievement yet further. Becoming effective in this second dimension may be a transformational process, as we have discussed earlier, in that it may require a different approach to the work of teaching. Even if it does not bring about transformation, it certainly requires that there is a continuous improvement orientation to the task of teaching. This requires a reflexive, reflective approach.

As we have argued in Chapter 4, the primary tasks of organisations are always associated with anxiety, and this is particularly the case in schools. The primary task of teaching and learning has a high level of emotion, particularly anxiety, associated with it. Improving the way in which a primary task is achieved will also have anxiety associated with it, as does all change. So changing the practice of teaching in an effort to improve it and to improve pupil achievement will also have anxiety associated with it. The containment of all this anxiety is an important role for the leaders of schools. This idea of anxiety containment is explored further in the next chapter.

THE LEADER'S WORK IN ENSURING EFFECTIVENESS AT THE DIFFERENT LEVELS

The leaders themselves   For the leaders, ensuring effectiveness means focusing on the task of leadership and being effective in improving their leadership practice. This work in turn requires leaders to occupy a boundary position in relation to the systems they lead. They must neither join the system (manifested by, for example, doing work that others can and should do) nor 'join' the environment. These actions would be social defences against undertaking the leadership role.

The leader in relation to others   With others, the leader must encourage them to focus on their primary task of first 'doing the job', then help them to improve what they do and even transform their sense of their role.

Leaders in relation to their institutions   The leader must also optimise effectiveness at an institutional level, ensuring that the institution is doing what it is supposed to do and doing it well, and being effective in *improving* what it is supposed to do. If this improvement process leads to a change in the way in which the school sees and experiences its role, the school will be transformed.

Leaders in relation to their institutions' key stakeholders   If the leader helps the institution's key stakeholders to be effective in accomplishing their primary tasks and being more effective in improving the way in which they carry out those primary tasks, it will help the leader's own institution to be effective.

Leadership optimises reflectivity

The last leadership principle is optimising reflectivity. Reflectivity is the capacity to reflect. For leadership purposes, reflectivity is primarily concerned with being aware of knowledge needs, seeking knowledge and using knowledge. Reflexivity in reflectivity is concerned with establishing the validity of knowledge.

THE LEADER'S WORK IN OPTIMISING REFLECTIVITY AT DIFFERENT LEVELS

The leaders themselves   At the level of the individual leader, reflectivity requires reflection *in* action in order to know the most appropriate response according the context. It also requires reflection *on* action to improve leadership practice. As discussed earlier, reflecting on action in a way that simply does not confirm inappropriate theories and actions usually requires the help of others, perhaps in a mentoring or supervisory role. Whether reflecting in or on action, the reflective process is still concerned with being aware of knowledge needs, seeking out that knowledge and using it appropriately, and continually ensuring and testing out the validity what is known.

The leaders in relation to others   With others, optimising reflectivity involves the leader in:

- adopting the role of enabling them to reflect appropriately
- helping others to be aware of their knowledge needs
- assisting them in the process of gaining knowledge
- supporting them as they use the knowledge they have and have acquired
- helping the other person to ensure the validity of their knowledge.

The leaders in relation to their institutions   Optimising reflectivity at the institutional level involves:

- facilitating the use of information, such as the institution's own performance and benchmarking data
- being aware of knowledge and information needs and what the institution's knowledge requirements are to ensure effectiveness and to improve
- ensuring that there are in place processes for seeking out and gathering knowledge
- ensuring that the processes and outcomes of it are valid, a key aspect of knowledge management.

The leaders in relation to their institutions' key stakeholders   Leaders must also work to enhance reflexive reflectivity in their institution's stakeholders, again assisting them with the four dimensions of being aware of knowledge needs, seeking knowledge, using knowledge, and ensuring that the processes and outcomes of reflection are valid.

The reflexive reflective practice of leadership will be framed, in part at least by the other leadership principles outlined here.

The ERA of educational leadership

These principles of leadership: Leading Educator; Adaptability; Direction, Direction, Destination; Effectiveness and Reflectivity give the convenient acronym of LEADER. The principles must be enacted at the four levels: the leaders themselves, and the leaders in relation to others; to their institutions; and their institutions' key stakeholders. The matrix created by the principles and levels provides a useful tool for the audit and development of leadership capability. Such an audit instrument, and some suggestions for its use, are given at the end of this chapter.

Of all of the leadership principles, optimising effectiveness, reflectivity and adaptability are crucial. The role of leading educator is in many ways the main role, overarching and subsuming the others and tying this model of leadership unequivocally to a learning model. The '3Ds of vision', which are having determination, having and giving direction, and knowing the destination, are key behaviours and capabilities. They are essential for – and implicit in – achieving the central tasks of good leadership. These central tasks are ensuring effectiveness, optimising reflectivity and optimising adaptability. So, the key leadership principles or themes are effectiveness, reflectivity and adaptability. Hence the acronym for the key educational leadership themes in this era of educational leadership is the ERA of educational leadership.

Assessing your leadership using the Leadership Principles

The Leadership Principles grid

There are five Leadership Principles

1	The Leadership as the:	Leading Educator
2	Leadership optimises:	Adaptability
3	Leadership has:	3D Vision
4	Leadership ensures:	Effectiveness
5	Leadership optimises:	Reflectivity

Each of these principles can be broken down in to different elements

1 The leader as the Leading Educator
   - the leading expert in the practice of education
   - the leading expert about education.

2   Leadership optimises **A**daptability
  - the ability to change
  - the motivation to change
  - opportunities to change.
3   3-**D** vision
  - determination
  - direction: knowing the direction, giving direction
  - destination.
4   Leadership ensures **E**ffectiveness
5   Leadership optimises **R**eflectivity
  - being aware of knowledge needs
  - seeking knowledge
  - using knowledge.

Your leadership will operate at different levels

1   *Yourself*
2   You in relation to *other individuals*
3   You in relation to *your institution* (that might be the whole school, a year group, a department, a curriculum grouping)
4   You in relation to *your institutions' key stakeholders*. To identify the key stakeholders think about all those who have an interest in your institution.

How to use the Leadership Principles Grid

The Leadership Principles Grid can be used in different ways.

1   Choose one of the principles and explore your leadership practice in that area, or
2   Choose one row and explore your practice in that sub-element of a particular principle, or
3   Choose one level (a column on the grid) and explore your leadership practice at that level, or
4   Choose one cell on the grid and explore your leadership practice in that specific area.

   To help you to consider your practice, here are some suggestions.

  - Ask yourself: 'What or who am I leading?' List the different groups, individuals, organisations and institutions. It will help to consider particular examples.
  - Think about specific examples, events or incidents. Refer back to specific examples: it will make the consideration of your leadership practice more realistic.

Leadership Principle	Leadership levels			
	Yourself	You and others	You and the institution	You and the institution's stakeholders
Leading Educator				
The leader as: The leading expert in the practice of education				
The leader as: The leading expert about education				
Leadership optimises Adaptability				
The leader optimises: The ability to change				
The leader optimises: The motivation to change				
The leader optimises: The opportunities to change				
Leadership has 3D vision				
The leader has: Determination				
The leader knows: The Direction				
The leader gives: Direction				
The leader knows: The Destination				
Leadership ensures Effectiveness				
The leader ensures: Effectiveness				
Leadership optimises Reflectivity				
The leader is: aware of knowledge needs				
The leader optimises: The seeking of knowledge				
The leader optimises: The use of knowledge				

Figure 9.2   The Leadership Principles Grid

- Think about improvement. When you have considered your practice, think how you could improve it. What might help you to improve? What are the barriers to improvement?
- Where are the 'no-go areas' in your leadership? Why are they there? How might you engage with them?

10 Some final considerations

Introduction

In this chapter, we attempt a final review of some of the key issues in the leadership of educational organisations and for that matter, leadership in all organisations. Although schools are special places with particular purposes, they have a great deal in common with all other organisations, so leadership in educational organisations will not be markedly different from leadership in any organisation.

In attempting to re-examine some key leadership issues and perhaps to home in on some of the crucial aspects of leadership, we run the risk of falling into the trap of simply listing 'leadership imperatives', a series of what 'good leaders' should do. None the less, despite that risk, we consider that it is worthwhile to set out some of the features of leadership, that perhaps go further than the list of characteristics and principles that we set out in Chapter 9. The particular themes are the central role of emotion in organising, leadership and the organisational roles of others, the integrating role of leadership, leadership and the containment of anxiety and leadership as reparation. We have deliberately set out these final considerations as propositions in order to make them as clear as possible. The intention is to provoke a debate about the points we are trying to make.

As with the leadership principles, this list is the consequence of a further interpretation of the data and our sense making of it in the light of the theoretical standpoint – institutional transformation – that we have taken in the book as a whole.

The central role of emotion in organising

In this book, we have argued that non-rational influences are the dominant force on the life of schools. Emotions, particularly anxiety, have a significant effect on the processes of organising and the structuring of organisations. Individuals and institutions will seek to defend themselves against the very real pain that difficult emotions can bring. Since many of these defences are driven by the unconscious in the individual and the collective unconscious in the institution, they can become part of the taken-for-granted fabric of organising. Emotion and the defences against it can therefore become major sources of organisational dysfunction. They influence the roles that individuals adopt. They impact on the way in which individuals enact their roles.

The influence is the result of:

- an individual's own experience of role-associated anxiety and her/his defences against it
- the projection of others' emotion and anxiety on to an individual
- the projection of institutional emotion and anxiety on to an individual.

All these influences shape an individual's role, affect the way a person takes up their role, and affect the way that role is enacted. Importantly emotions, especially anxiety, play a major part in shaping the gap between the espoused role and the in-use role. The experience of emotion can bring the espoused and in use roles together, and it can drive them apart. Arguably, the gap must be closed if the individual, the group and the institution are to flourish.

Leadership and the organisational roles of others

It is a truism that leadership is important in institutions and in all organisations that have a purpose. When we think about organisations and roles within organisations, it is obvious that leadership is a special role, in that its purpose is to enable others, both individuals and groupings such as departments and teams, to take up and to enact their roles effectively. In doing that, leadership must:

- define the roles
- set out the purposes of roles
- help to make clear and assist the management of the boundaries of roles
- create the organisational conditions that enable roles to be taken up and enacted.

As leadership actions, these imperatives are relatively straightforward. They are managerial and contractual in nature, they help others to do work productively and effectively in an organisation, they are transactional. To carry through a more fundamental change in an institution such as a school, the leader must bring about a change in the way in which others and the institution itself see their roles. This fundamental change requires a much deeper shift in individuals and the various sub-systems in the institution and the institution itself. As we discussed in Chapter 9, it calls for a transformation and for transformational leadership to bring it about.

Three further propositions relate to this consideration of leadership and the organisational roles of others.

1   Enabling others to take up their roles and enact them in either a transactional or a transformational way cannot be done without the use of power. The effective leader uses power to influence others.
2   From the perspective on leadership that we have taken, it is easy to understand the attractiveness of notions of dispersed, shared, or participatory leadership in educational organisations, or any organisation for that matter. Just imagine how powerful an organisation might be if every member of the organisation, in addition to their own organisational role, had a leadership role in enabling all the other members of the organisation to take up and to enact their roles.
3   On a more general point, there is a case for arguing that our interpretation of the meaning of leadership is the very essence of organising in educational institutions and other organisations. Effective organising is about enabling others to take up and enact a role that contributes to the purpose of the organisation.

The integrating role of leadership

In addition to the role of enabling others to take up and enact their roles, leadership has a role as integrator in the institution. Again, this role operates at two levels, the transactional and the transformational. At the transactional level, leadership is primarily concerned with ensuring that the various individuals and groups, in their different roles work together in harmony to achieve the organisation's purposes. Ensuring harmonious working is particularly important in educational organisations because of the integrated nature of the various activities of the institution. For example, in a secondary school, it is crucial that 'pastoral' and 'curricular' teams work together. In primary schools it is crucial for the progression of pupils that the different teachers in their year-teaching role follow a curriculum that ensures appropriate pupil progression. The integrating role of leadership at the transactional level ensures that there is:

*   *clarity* in the various individuals and groups about how their particular roles relate to those of other individuals and groups
*   *compatibility* between the different roles, so that individuals and groups can take up and enact their roles without inappropriate conflict with other individuals and groups
*   *concord*, so that the various individuals and groups agree and understand how their roles relate to those of other individuals and groups.

This transactional integration is not predicated on a belief that there will be no conflict in the organisation. Nor is it based on a view that conflict will be absent, as the integration that has been achieved has to be adapted during organisational change. There will always be conflict in organising, but it is leadership's role in the process of integration to mediate and resolve conflicts.

At another level, the transformational level, the integrator role can achieve a higher order outcome. At this higher level, leadership seeks to:

- add value to the role-related activities of the various individuals and groups within and outwith the institution, by seeing how the activities of the different groups can mutually enhance the activities of other individuals and groups
- create synergy so that through the process of groups and individuals working together, the outcomes of the whole are greater than the sum of the parts
- enable networking, collaboration and partnership activities to take place successfully.

Leadership in the integrator role can and arguably must be undertaken by the *ex officio* head of the organisation, for example, the headteacher of a school. That assertion however does not preclude any individual or group within the organisation undertaking an integration role.

Leadership and the containment of anxiety

To confirm, a key aspect of leadership is the containment of anxiety of other groups and individuals. Anxiety containment is the task in the following illustrations.

- Anxiety containment is an important role for class teachers as they lead the learning of their pupils. They have to contain the anxiety as the learners take up their roles as learners, and the anxiety inherent in learning and change.
- Leaders must contain the anxiety of others as they help them take up and enact their organisational roles. This anxiety-containment role is essential because taking up a work role always has emotion, and therefore anxiety, associated with it. Containing this role-related anxiety is a particularly difficult task in educational leadership because of the anxiety-laden nature of teaching.
- Individuals, groups and the whole institution will experience anxiety as they change the way they see their role because change always has anxiety associated with it. Leaders must contain the anxiety that is associated with change.

The containment of anxiety takes place in two important ways. The first is to set boundaries and structures within and around phenomena and events, especially those that involve significant change, in order to limit anxiety associated with them. Containing anxiety in this way is an important leadership task and a responsibility for the leader. Second, leaders are the temporary (ideally) recipients of the anxiety projected towards them by those they are leading. Leadership is the place where difficult feelings created by the organisation and change in the organisation can be 'offloaded' and held. Again, this containment is an important leadership task and responsibility. However, if the containment of projected emotion and anxiety is permanent or even semi-permanent, the leadership task may become unbearable. Again, the burdensome nature of the containment of projected anxiety may be one explanation as to why shared leadership is an attractive notion. It spreads the burden of projected anxiety.

Leadership as reparation

The importance of vision in leadership in our explorations of educational change is one of the strong themes to emerge in our study. Vision, defined as determination, direction and destination, is one of the leadership principles, and the importance of vision in leadership is well established. Interestingly, in many of the schools we studied, the vision appeared to go deeper. In our discussions with the headteachers in particular, we were struck by the pride – fully justified – that many of them had in what they and their colleagues had achieved, by the scale of the achievement and by the apparent personal cost to some of them. The accounts were often genuinely touching.

Many of the schools we worked with had started from a very low base and had experienced a number of problems and challenges in the early stages of their journeys. One way of interpreting what the leaders of these improvement journeys had achieved was that they had led the 'repair' of the institutions for which they were responsible. In a variety of ways, including importantly the dismantling of inappropriate social defences and reintegrating the separated parts, they had intuitively engaged in what Melanie Klein (Segal 1979) called the process of reparation. Klein has made reparation one of the foundations of her developmental interpretation of human life. She argued that through art and creative acts, we help to fashion artefacts of completeness, wholeness and beauty. Klein suggested that the act of artistic creation helps to complete and repair any sense of fragmentation in the person's inner world, and also enables the recipients of the art to feel complete and satisfied. In a way, by creating 'new' schools, the leaders of the change created a work of art. They had in a sense repaired their institutions. They had restored a sense of completeness and wholeness to their institutions, and, arguably, had created in educational terms an object of beauty. In many of the leaders, the energy to create these repaired institutions appeared to have a deep origin, and may have been driven by a desire to effect some kind of inner reparation. Certainly many of the recipients of their art, for example the pupils, parents and the wider community, benefited and experienced a sense of satisfaction from what these leaders had created. This institutional-reparation interpretation of leadership action may give some insight into the enormous commitment that many of these headteachers and teachers had to their work of recreating their schools.

Appendix
The work undertaken by the project to enhance collaboration

One of the important aims of the project was to promote and facilitate the sharing of experience *among* schools as they strived to improve the progress and achievements of their pupils. This promotion of collaboration was achieved in a number of ways. They are summarised as follows.

The Interim Project Conference   In October 1997, a conference was held to disseminate initial research findings, and provide a forum for the exchange of ideas and networking.

Networking   The project facilitated a number of linkages between schools and colleagues who have shared interests or are undertaking similar improvement initiatives.

Collaboration between the primary and secondary phases and between education authorities   Cross-phase and cross-authority collaboration can offer benefits to all schools. The project worked mostly with primary schools in the development of a model inter-school collaboration. Working with primary schools provided useful experience on the development of a model for cross-authority networking. A useful starting point was to provide all of the schools with some basic information about one another before networking could begin. To this end, a profile was prepared on each of the participating schools, based on successful improvement initiatives and school development plan priorities identified by each of the schools. At subsequent cross-authority networking sessions, participants (mostly headteachers) identified common interests and planned future development activities. The two special schools involved in the project were also participants in the Primary Network.

Workshops   The project facilitated a number of workshops in which practitioners shared good practice. During a four-month period, five schools held workshops either during the day, where colleagues could observe the initiative in action, or more commonly, after school. These sessions, which were well planned and delivered by school staff, proved to be valuable opportunities for teachers to share successful improvement initiatives and to help and support one another. In many cases, the workshops were followed up when the schools concerned received further requests for information and additional visits from individual or groups of teachers who had been unable to attend the initial sessions. During this period, approximately 350 teachers were involved in workshop and/or follow-up activities.

School Improvement Bulletin   Funding provided by the Mid Glamorgan and Gwent Training and Enterprise Councils (TECs) has enabled the project, in conjunction with ESIS, to publish a *School Improvement Bulletin*. The Bulletin is distributed each term to *all* schools within the four authorities. Most of the articles are written by practitioners, and describe their personal involvement in the process of school improvement. The response to the initiative was very positive. During the project, an increasing number of teachers came forward with accounts of their own involvement in an activity which has had an impact on raising standards in one form or another. Many teachers may not see what they are doing as part of their professional commitment as significant. Positive feedback from those who read the bulletin indicates that this is not the case. Teachers who read the bulletin indicate that the reports encourage other colleagues. Publication and distribution of the bulletin also result in networking with other school improvement projects further afield. This sharing of good practice results in more teachers coming to know about the ways in which fellow professionals operate effectively. This process of sharing good practice is likely to lead to improved practice generally.

Use of case studies   The development of case studies was an important part of the project's work. The case studies represent teachers' own efforts to improve their practice and have been found to be useful in the development of an applied learning and enquiry approach. Potential authors were provided with a framework for writing that helped to ensure that they included sufficient information on the main issues arising at the initiation, implementation and institutional stages of the initiative. Initially a number of the authors expressed their concern at writing for others, but by completion they reported that the activity had been worthwhile. Their confidence in writing about their experiences improved, but more importantly, it was felt that the involvement of staff in critically reflecting on their practice had been very beneficial. In all of their accounts, we believe, it is possible to hear the teacher's voice. This enhances their value, relevance and sense of realism.

A conference to disseminate the findings of the project   was held in January 1999.

Annotated bibliography

This section gives very brief summaries of some of the key texts in the fields covered by the book. Among them, are texts that have informed our thinking, shaped our first thoughts, and helped to make sense of the improvement stories we heard and recorded. It is by no means a comprehensive list of all the texts that are available on organisational change in education and other settings, and the underlying forces and motives that influence the process of organising. All the texts in this bibliography are recommended reading for those who are interested in educational leadership, educational change, the influence of the unconscious in organisations, and institutional transformation. The texts are listed in alphabetical order of the first author's surname.

French, R.and Vince, R. (1999) *Group Relations, Management and Organisation*, Oxford: Oxford University Press.

This is an excellent text. The editors have assembled chapters from leading international figures in the field that explore the theory and practice of group relations. The various chapters explore and analyse the influences of the unconscious on the behaviour of those who manage in work organisations. As such, the book gives fresh insights into the difficult but often more real side of organisational life. From the group relations perspective, the authors examine the issues of managing and resisting change, leadership, anxiety and stress, identity and the 'inner world' of organisations. This book is essential reading for those who have an interest in the influence of the unconscious on organisational processes.

Fullan, M. (1991) *The New Meaning of Educational Change*, London: Cassell.

This classic work follows on from Fullan's first major educational change text, *The Meaning of Educational Change*. The book's strengths are its comprehensiveness, its analysis of the objective and subjective dimensions of educational change, and its consideration of the multiple perspectives on change. It is in three parts. The first reviews educational change, its complexity and its different stages. The second section reflects on change at the local level, while the third builds on that perspective to consider change at the regional and national levels.

Fullan, M. (1993) *Change Forces: Probing the Depths of Educational Reform*, London: Falmer.

A text that is written with energy and verve, and its vitality gives it an inspirational feel. Michael Fullan tackles head-on some of the key issues in educational change. He first addresses the problematics of educational change, before going on to explore the moral purpose of educational change and the role of those helping the change process. He then considers schools as learning organisations, the learning organisation and its environment, and teacher education. A final chapter explores the individual and the learning society, where he argues that the purpose of education is not only to produce a learning society but a 'learning globe'.

Gray, J., Hopkins, D., Reynolds, D., Wilcox, B., Farrell, S. and Jesson, D. (1999) *Improving Schools*, Oxford: Oxford University Press.

This text draws on research funded by the Economic and Social Research Council to explore change processes in schools. The research analysed schools over a five-year period. The schools were wide-ranging in type and faced serious challenges. The highly stimulating and readable text first explores the frameworks and assumptions underpinning the notion of school improvement. There are then case studies of the various schools, which explore significant themes in the change processes. The final section analyses and discusses the more general aspects of the change process, including the starting points of change, patterns of change, and building the capacity to change in order to improve pupil achievement.

Harris, A., Bennett, N. and Preedy, M. (eds) (1997) *Organisational Effectiveness in Education*, Buckingham: Open University Press.

This is a collection of key texts in organisation, effectiveness and improvement in education. Almost all the chapters are significant, previously published journal articles or important chapters from other texts. It is therefore invaluable. The papers are grouped into three sections. The first covers organisational theory and analysis, the second covers theory, research and practice in school and college effectiveness, and the third covers managing change for school and college improvement. The book's stated intention, which it achieves, is to provide an understanding of the way in which organisational effectiveness is conceptualised, measured and realised. It also provides a very useful review of the ways in which change for organisational improvement can be managed in practice. The articles, are well chosen, and the ideas and theoretical concepts are readily accessible.

Hickman, G. R. (ed.) (1998) *Leading Organisations: Perspectives for a New Era*, London: Sage.

This is an exceptional text containing over fifty key chapters on leadership by eminent authors in the field. All the chapters have been published previously, either as journal articles or as chapters in leadership texts. One of the strengths of the text is the framework within which the various chapters are grouped. This framework includes the changing environment of twenty-first century organisations, the assessment of changes in the external environment, understanding and incorporating the organisational context and requirements, the contribution of leaders and organisational members, the move towards mission, creating viable structures, aligning goals with vision and mission, framing culture, building capacity, and the contribution of organisations to society.

Hirschhorn, L. (1997) *The Workplace Within*, London: MIT Press.

The subtitle to this excellent text – *The Psychodynamics of Organisational Life* – very appropriately describes its focus. There are four sections. The first section explores social defences, boundaries and the psychodynamics of taking a role. The second section comprises two case studies, the first of which explores covert coalitions, while the second speculates on management training as a social defence. In the third section Hirschhorn contemplates the breakdown of social defences in what he terms the post-industrial milieu. The final section is an in-depth exploration of work and reparation. In this section, Hirschhorn rightly takes an optimistic stance on the potential for workplaces and the engagement in 'good work' to engender developmental cultures in work organisations.

Joyce, B., Calhoun, E. and Hopkins, D. (1999) *The New Structure of School Improvement: Inquiring Schools and Achieving Students*, Milton Keynes: Open University Press.

A comprehensive and highly relevant text that extends the earlier work of Joyce and his colleagues, *The Structure of School Improvement* published in 1983. The book covers a remarkable amount of ground encompassing schools as centres of enquiry and development, the detailed practice of school improvement, and educational change and policy-making for school renewal. It is well written and authoritative in style. One of its strengths is the way in which it draws on insights and experience from both sides of the Atlantic. This an excellent text, which contains numerous case studies, data of all kinds and the authors' considerable experience in working with, schools. It is also highly readable and engaging in its style and approach.

Kets de Vries, M. (ed.) (1991) *Organisations on the Couch: Clinical Perspectives on Organisational Behaviour and Change,* San Francisco: Jossey-Bass.

There are numerous insights into some of the non-rational explanations of behaviour in organisations in this text. It explores the ways in which unconscious processes can shape an organisation's strategy and character. The seventeen chapters, all of them original pieces by leading authors, cover alternative perspectives on organisations, leadership, change processes in work groups, the factors that influence organisational character, and organisational consultation and change. There are in-depth case studies that illustrate the experience of organisations and leadership in both the private and public sectors. The book is fascinating reading for the insights it gives into culture, leadership and organisation.

McNiff, J. (1988) *Action Research: Principles and Practice,* Basingstoke: Macmillan.

This book remains both an excellent explanation of action research and a guide to carrying out action research projects. The text is grounded in education and is therefore of particular use to those who are contemplating undertaking action research in educational settings. The first part gives a very useful background to action research, explaining what it is and its limitations, discussing action research as an educational tradition, and describing some of the different approaches to educational action research. This first part also explains why teachers should engage in action research. The second part deals with the practical aspects of carrying out an action research study, and is divided into guidance on the research process and useful illustrative case studies. The final section explores some of the wider implications of action research, with chapters that explore claims to validity, the in-service education and training of teachers, and using networks and networking to support action research.

Morrison, K. (1998) *Management Theories for Educational Change,* London: Paul Chapman.

This very useful text reviews the major theories and perspectives on organisational change. As such it covers from an educational standpoint all the main themes in the change and organisation behaviour literature.

The first part deals with the macro-contexts of change, and the second, the micro-contexts. In the first part there are chapters on the nature of change, managing change from a Japanese perspective, and quality management. In the second part there are sections on responses of individuals to change, organisational factors in the change process, teamwork and leadership.

Obholzer, A. and Zagier Roberts, V. (eds) (1994) *The Unconscious at Work,* London: Routledge.

Drawing on ideas from psychoanalysis, open systems theory, the work of Wilfrid Bion and group relations training, this book provides an excellent overview of the influence of the unconscious in work organisations. The first four chapters present a highly readable introduction to the key ideas, which together form a helpful theoretical framework. The remaining sections largely comprise case studies written by present or past members of the Tavistock Clinic Consulting to Institutions Workshop. The case studies, which are largely drawn from care settings such as schools, hospitals and community care settings, serve to illustrate the main themes outlined in the earlier sections. It is an excellent read and is highly recommended.

Schein, E. H. (1992) *Organisational Culture and Leadership,* San Francisco: Jossey Bass.

A classic text that addresses the complex interplay between leadership and organisational culture. It builds on the first edition, published in the 1980s, by focusing more on the processes of organisational change. The first part explores the nature of culture, what it is, what is does, its various dimensions, and the study and interpretation of culture. The later parts are devoted to exploring the interaction of leadership and culture, and draw on numerous vignettes and case study material. The book is a fascinating read and contains numerous insights into leadership, change and culture.

Senge, P. (1990) *The Fifth Discipline: The Art and Practice of the Learning Organisation,* London: Century Business.

A highly influential text that remains very relevant reading for all those who are interested in organisational change regardless of the setting. The book attempts to shift thinking about leadership, organisation and change. Senge identifies what he calls the 'component technologies' that provide the essential elements of organisations. These are 'Systems Thinking', as a vehicle for making sense of organisational complexity; 'Personal Mastery', which is the discipline of continually clarifying and deepening personal vision, 'Mental Models', the taken-for-granted assumptions, pictures and images that influence our thoughts and actions; 'Building a Shared Vision' to develop shared images of the future, to nurture genuine commitment and engagement; and 'Team Learning', which is the way in which the various groups in the organisation link up, talk and learn. Senge considers that it is this 'Team Learning' that is vital to success.

Stoll, L. and Fink, D. (1996) *Changing our Schools,*
Buckingham: Open University Press.

This is one of the most helpful texts on 'what makes a good school', and is required reading for anyone who is serious about changing schools to improve pupil achievement. The book is based on a school improvement project based in the Halton school district of Ontario, and the numerous insights are grounded in the authors experiences of working on that project. The chapters in the book cover school development planning, leadership, teaching and learning, the need for partnerships, building a learning community, and evaluation. The book is well written, accessible, and highly relevant to practice in schools.

Yukl, G. (1998) *Leadership in Organisations*, New Jersey:
Prentice-Hall.

In this very comprehensive text, all the major aspects of leadership are covered. There are sections that explore the nature of leadership, the different perspectives on leadership such as leadership behaviour, leadership traits and skills, contingency theories, charismatic leadership and transformational leadership. There are also chapters that consider leader – follower relations, leadership of teams, leadership development and the role of the leaders in managing change. Yukl uses numerous case studies to illustrate the various ideas, although these are typically set in commercial/industrial contexts. In this excellent and readable text, Yukl draws on almost a thousand references form the leadership literature.

References

Bacharach, S. B. and Lawler, E. J. (1998) 'Political alignments in organisations: contextualisation, mobilisation and co-ordination', in R. M. Kramer and M. A. Neale (eds), *Power and Influence in Organisations*, London: Sage.

Bass, B. M. (1996) *Handbook of Leadership: A Survey of Theory and Research*, New York: Free Press.

Bion, W. (1961) *Experiences in Groups*, New York: Basic Books.

Burns, J. M. (1978) *Leadership*, New York: Harper and Row.

Connor, D. R. (1995) *Managing at the Speed of Change: How Resilient Managers Succeed and Prosper where Others Fail*, New York: Villard.

Everard, K. B. and Morris, G. (1985) *Effective School Management*, London: Harper and Row.

Fullan, M. (1991) *The New Meaning of Educational Change*, London: Cassell.

—— (1993) *Change Forces*, London: Falmer.

Gabriel, Y. (1999) *Organisations in Depth*, London: Sage.

Hardy, C. (1994) *Mobilising Strategic Action*, London: Sage.

Hickman, G. R. (ed.) (1998) *Leading Organizations: Perspectives for a New Era*, London: Sage.

Hirschhorn, L. (1990) *The Workplace Within*, London: MIT Press.

Hopkins, D., Ainscow, M., and West, M. (1994) *School Improvement in an Era of Change*, London: Cassell.

Hopkins, D., West, M. and Ainscow, M. (1996) 'School improvement – propositions for action', in A. Harris, N. Bennett and M. Preedy (eds), *Organisational Effectiveness and Improvement in Education*, Buckingham: Open University Press.

Institute of Education (1994) *Research Matters*, no. 1 (Summer), London: Institute of Education School Improvement Network.

Jones, G. N. (1968) Planned Organisational Change, London: Routledge and Kegan Paul.

Kanter, R. M., Stein, B. A. and Jick, T. J. (1992) *The Challenge of Organisational Change*, New York: Free Press.

MacGilchrist, B., Myers, K. and Reed, J. (1997) *The Intelligent School*, London: Paul Chapman.

McNiff, J. (1988) *Action Research Principles and Practice*, Basingstoke: Macmillan.

Meyerson, D. and Martin, J. (1987) 'Cultural change: an integration of three different views', *Journal of Management* 24: 623–47.

Morrison, K. (1998) *Management Theories for Educational Change*, London: Paul Chapman.

Obholzer, A. and Zagier Roberts, V. (eds) (1994) *The Unconscious at Work*, London: Routledge.

Pettigrew, A. M., McKee, L. and Ferlie, E. (1988) 'Understanding change in the NHS', *Public Administration* 66: 297–317.

Rosenholtz, S. (1989) *Teachers' Workplace: The Social Organisation of Schools*, New York: Longman.

Rost, J. C. (1991) *Leadership for the Twenty-First Century*, Westport, Conn.: Greenwood.

—— (1998) 'Leadership and management', in G. R. Hickman (ed.), *Leading Organisations: Perspectives for a New Era*, London: Sage.

Sammons, P., Hillman, J. and Mortimore, P. (1995) *Key Characteristics of Effective Schools: A Review of School Effectiveness and Research*, London: Office for Standards in Education.

Schon, D. A. (1983) *The Reflective Practitioner*, New York: Basic Books.

Segal, H. (1979) *Melanie Klein*, New York: Viking.

Senge, P. (1990) *The Fifth Discipline: The Art and Practice of the Learning Organisation,* London: Century Business.

Stoll, L. and Fink, D. (1996) *Changing our Schools: Linking School Effectiveness and School Improvement*, Milton Keynes: Open University Press.

Welsh Office (1997) *Building Excellent Schools Together,* Cardiff: Welsh Office.

van Velzen, W., Miles, M., Eckholm, M., Hameyer, U. and Robin, D. (1985) *Making School Improvement Work*, Leuven: ACCO.

Vince, R. and Martin, L. (1993) 'Inside action learning: the psychology and the politics of the action learning model', *Management Education and Development* 24 (3): 205–15.

Whitehead, J. (1989) 'Creating a living educational theory from questions of the kind, 'How do I improve my practice?' *Cambridge Journal of Education* 19 (1): 41–52.

Wilson, D. C. (1992). *A Strategy of Change: Concepts and Controversies in the Management of Change*, London: Routledge.

Yukl, G. (1994) *Leadership in Organisations*. Englewood Cliffs, N.Y.: Prentice Hall.

Index